Smoke & SPICE

Smoke & SPICE

Recipes for **SEASONINGS**, *rubs*, **MARINADES**, **BRINES**, *glazes* & **BUTTERS**

Valerie **AIKMAN-SMITH**

PHOTOGRAPHY BY *Erin* KUNKEL

LONDON • NEW YORK

Designer Geoff Borin
Editor Rebecca Woods
Senior Production Controller Toby Marshall
Art Director Leslie Harrington
Editorial Director Julia Charles

Food Stylist Valerie Aikman-Smith
Prop Stylist Jennifer Barguiarena
Indexer Hilary Bird

First published in 2013 by
Ryland Peters & Small
20–21 Jockey's Fields
London WC1R 4BW
and
519 Broadway, 5th Floor
New York, NY 10012

www.rylandpeters.com

10 9 8 7 6 5 4 3 2

Text © Valerie Aikman-Smith 2013

Design and photographs © Ryland Peters & Small 2013

ISBN: 978-1-84975-350-0

A CIP record for this book is available from the British Library.

US Library of Congress CIP data has been applied for.

Printed in China

Notes:

• All spoon measurements are level unless otherwise specified.

• All eggs are large (UK) or extra large (US), unless otherwise specified.

• Ovens should be preheated to the specified temperatures. We recommend using an
oven thermometer. If using a fan-assisted oven, adjust temperatures according to the
manufacturer's instructions.

• Weights and measurements have been rounded up or down slightly to make
measuring easier.

• To sterilize preserving jars, wash them in hot, soapy water and rinse in boiling water.
Place in a large saucepan and cover with hot water. With the saucepan lid on, bring
the water to a boil and continue boiling for 15 minutes. Turn off the heat and leave
the jars in the hot water until just before they are to be filled. Invert the jars onto a
clean dish towel to dry. Sterilize the lids for 5 minutes, by boiling or according to the
manufacturer's instructions. Jars should be filled and sealed while they are still hot.

• When a recipe calls for the grated zest of lemons or limes or uses slices of fruit, buy
unwaxed fruit and wash well before using. If you can only find treated fruit, scrub well
in warm soapy water before using.

CONTENTS

INTRODUCTION

When you open your pantry door and reach for a simple everyday spice, have you ever stopped and thought how the contents of this small jar had led to the discovery of new lands and peoples?

Venice monopolized the spice trade due to it's location and connections in the East and in the 1400's Europe searched for faster and safer sailing routes there. Columbus discovered the West Indies believing he had discovered the East Indies, and the Portuguese rounded the Cape of Good Hope, stopping at Cape Town on their way to India.

Spices were precious and sought after, not just for cooking, but also used in medicines, ceremonies, perfumes, and incense. If you have walked through a souk and breathed in the heady heavenly spices and admired the kaleidoscope of colors, you will understand their powers and why we use them so much.

The spice routes have been around for as long as mankind and spices were used as currency to buy and barter with. It is said that the Queen of Sheba brought spices to King Solomon and Cleopatra bewitched Caesar with these aromatics.

Seasonings and spices began to be used in cooking, and as a way to preserve food after it had been hunted and gathered, long before our modern technology of refrigeration and freezing. They helped hide the taste of food that was well past it's best and to make it edible. They also preserved foods for when times were meager and hunting was lean.

These days we are fortunate to have spice stores dedicated to selling fabulous fragrant and pungent mixes. The local supermarkets have shelves filled with these wonderfully scented cooking condiments. Look out for Fair Trade labels and buy where possible, ensuring good practices. Most towns have fresh farmers' markets selling local organic produce.

Buy locally sustainable organic meats and produce. It makes a huge difference and buying from local farmers helps the local economy and encourages great farming practices. Get to know your purveyors—it can be a lot of fun finding out their sources and they always have recipes to share.

If you are lucky enough to live in the countryside, where farm stands are dotted, even better. A lot of people are now growing their own, from a pot of herbs on their balcony, to raised beds in the back yard to community gardens. Bring home your bounty, get into the kitchen, and start mixing up some seasonings to make a wonderful afternoon lunch of grilled market veggies. Gather friends together and whip up a marinade, fire up the barbecue, and get grilling.

A quick note about grills/barbecues. The recipes for grilled dishes in this book have been tested on gas grills/barbecues, but can easily be cooked over coals, too—simply adjust the cooking times up or down, as appropriate.

SPICE MIXES give you the chance to become daring as there are no hard-and-fast rules—just have fun playing around and inventing new combinations. They can have just a few ingredients or a laundry list, and you can customize them to your taste. A great tip for getting the most flavor from your spices is to roast them for a few minutes in a hot dry pan over a medium–high heat to bring out all the aromatics. When cool, store the spice mixes in small glass jars with tight-fitting lids to keep them fresh, but don't keep them for more than 6 months as the spices will begin to lose their flavour.

MARINADES seem to be the most commonly used way to season food, especially in summer when the grill/barbecue is pulled out and dusted down for the grilling season. They not only flavor but tenderize food too, especially larger pieces of meat or cheaper cuts, which work well on a hot grill. Marinades always contain some kind of acid, whether it's vinegar or citrus juices, such as lemons, limes, or grapefruit, which help tenderize the meats. They are perfect for everything and the longer you can marinade the food the better it will taste. However, you can only marinade fish for 30 minutes as the acids start to cook the fish. The only exception to this is ceviche, where you do want the seafood to be cooked in the acidic juices.

BRINING is an excellent way to get flavor into foods, especially poultry and pork, which take on the flavors easily. Brining can take from 2 hours to 5 days depending on the meat. Brines need to be cold before placing the food in them, so be prepared and start ahead. Once you have tried it and tasted the difference you will see how easy it really is.

RUBS are a constant in our house. I make up concoctions and store them in glass jars ready to use at a moment's notice. They give a great layer of seasoning on poultry and meat. They can be made up of a mixture of dry spices or fresh herbs or both. I like to score the skin of chicken, then sprinkle and rub in.

PASTES are simply rubs that have had oils, wines, or vinegars added and mixed until you have a thick paste. They land somewhere between a marinade and a rub. This can be a quick solution if you don't have time to marinade as they give instant flavor.

GLAZES are a wonderful way to season and at the same time help protect the outside of meat, allowing it to remain juicy and tender. They normally have some kind of sugar element such as jam, honey, or maple syrup, which not only taste great but give cooked foods a wonderful glossy shimmer, especially on baked hams.

BUTTERS are so simple to make. Use unsalted butter as you can mix and match different flavored salts to the season. I like to make seasonal butter, especially when it's truffle season, and freeze in the shape of a log, so I can slice off bits as I need them. Rub flavored butters under the skin of poultry and it will give a crispy skin and juicy meat.

CREAMS are quick and easy to prepare and take on any kind of spice, fruit, or savory seasoning that you care to make. Dolloped on desserts or cold smoked salmon, they are divine.

PORK

Most people will say that pork is their favorite meat, especially bacon—well, what's not great about bacon? Salty sweet and smoked, it livens up any dish. But bacon is just a small part of a pig which offers so many delicious cuts to eat.

Try to always buy local, organic, and sustainable pork. There is a huge difference in taste and it keeps the industry of raising pork humane. If you are lucky enough to live near a farm that raises pigs in a sustainable manner, then get your pork from there. Ask your local butcher where he sources his meat and what the history is. Most of us, however, have to rely on the pork at our local supermarket and in this case you should always buy organic.

Several breeds of pig are now widely available and all have their own unique flavors. Heritage pigs, such as Berkshire, Tamworth, and Yorkshire, are showing up at local butchers so if you can, try different breeds and be adventurous, choosing cuts that you may not be as familiar with and asking the butcher how to prepare them. They will always have a recipe tucked up their sleeves.

Then there are the more expensive breeds, such as the free-roaming black Iberico pig. They are found in the southwestern part of Spain in a region called the Dehesa, where there is an abundance of oak trees—pigs love acorns. The ham that comes from these pigs is called Pata Negra and the fat is alleged to have the same qualities as olive oil. It is very expensive but well worth the experience.

I'm sure you know the expression "snout-to-tail" and some people do it very well, but for the average person, the more well known cuts of meat are what they would like to cook.

The shoulder cut is a less expensive piece and needs to be roasted or braised slowly and at a low heat, allowing it to tenderize as it cooks. This piece of the pig also has a higher fat content, which allows for a very tender, juicy piece of meat when cooked—perfect for pulled pork sandwiches.

The loin and tenderloin are more expensive cuts of meat and have no marbling of fat in them. The loin can be stuffed and roasted and will serve quite a few people, whereas the tenderloin is smaller and skinnier piece and is delicious for stir fries.

Pork ribs need to be marinated for as long as possible before grilling. Pork soaks up flavors so all kind of marinades and rubs can be used, whether it's a fiery chili bbq sauce or a herbed Mediterranean style, you won't be disappointed. Even though this all seems like a long process, when you start to eat them straight off the grill/barbecue and the meat is falling off the bone, it feels like the best day of your life.

Pork belly is layered with fat and meat and when brined and smoked makes bacon. Chinese or Cajun crispy pork belly is always a treat to eat, rich and intensely flavored. Pork belly takes on brines, rubs, and marinades with gusto. You can finely chop it and use in soups and salads.

Of course, bacon goes with everything, thickly or thinly sliced. You can eat it in a sandwich, wrap it around chickens and pieces of meat, or chop it up and sprinkle it over salads or a simple baked potato. Cook it with eggs as a leisurely weekend breakfast while reading the papers.

In this chapter there are several ways to prepare pork that you will enjoy over and over again and add to your collection of favorite dishes.

Smoky CHILI BBQ SAUCE

1 cup/240 ml molasses

1 cup/240 ml tomato ketchup

1 cup/240 ml maple syrup

2 chipotle chiles in adobo sauce

2 Jalapeño chiles, roughly chopped

2 scallions/spring onions, roughly chopped

2 roasted red bell peppers

1 yellow onion, roughly chopped

4 garlic cloves, peeled and bashed

a 3-inch/7-cm piece fresh ginger, peeled and roughly chopped

freshly squeezed juice of 1 lemon

a large bunch of fresh cilantro/coriander leaves, roughly chopped

sea salt and cracked black pepper

YIELDS 2½ CUPS/600 ML

When I make marinades, I tend to open the pantry door and make a sauce of what is in there, using up half jars of this and that. However, my stay fast ingredients are always smoky chipotle peppers in adobo sauce, maple syrup, and ginger, which make a wonderful sticky sauce for ribs.

Put all the ingredients in a blender or food processor and process until you have a smooth sauce.

Store the marinade in an airtight container in the fridge for up to 2 weeks.

To use, put the meat in a ceramic dish, pour over the sauce, and leave to marinate for 8–24 hours in the fridge. Let the meat come to room temperature, then cook according to the recipe on page 14, or as preferred. This sauce also works well with beef and poultry.

Hogwild Bourbon GLAZE

½ cup/120 ml bourbon
(such as Wild Turkey)

2 tablespoons molasses

1 tablespoon honey

½ teaspoon chipotle chili powder

2 garlic cloves, peeled and
roughly chopped

2 tablespoons chunky orange
marmalade

2 tablespoons olive oil

1 sprig fresh rosemary

sea salt and ground black pepper

YIELDS 1 CUP/240 ML

I have fallen hard for the South through the wonderful ingredients and foods they have—all seemingly dark, heady flavors with a burst of fruit somewhere. Whether it's peach, apples, or quinces, it's always a nice surprise. Bourbon is a regular in many dishes and I use Wild Turkey bourbon from Kentucky, firstly because I love the name and secondly because it tastes great.

Put all the ingredients in a blender or food processor and process until puréed and smooth.

Store the glaze in an airtight container in the fridge for up to 2 weeks.

Use according to the recipe on page 17, or marinate bacon, chops, ribs, and pork roasts in the glaze overnight, then remove from the glaze and cook, as preferred. Simmer the remaining glaze for 10 minutes to reduce, then serve on the side of the cooked meat.

Hog Heaven SPICE MIX

2 tablespoons dried sage

1 tablespoon dried thyme

1 teaspoon dried lemon peel

1 teaspoon dried garlic powder

1 teaspoon coarse sea salt

1 teaspoon ground white pepper

YIELDS GENEROUS ¼ CUP/
4½ TABLESPOONS

As the name suggests, this is one of my spice mixes that came about because of my love of anything pig. Use this as a basic rub or add olive oil to it and make it into a paste.

Put all the ingredients in a bowl and mix together.

Store the spice mix in a glass jar with a tight-fitting lid for up to 6 months.

To use, rub the spices over the pork and cook as preferred. Alternatively, add 1 tablespoon of the spice mix to ½ cup/120 ml olive oil and use as a dip for crusty breads.

Sticky SMOKY
BBQ RIBS

Sticky, finger lickin' ribs are so much fun to eat. You get to use your hands and no one is judging your manners as you tear into them with sauce flying everywhere. They are made for outdoor eating. Make sure you slowly cook them so the meat is just falling off the bones.

Wash the ribs under cold water and pat dry with a paper towel. Put the ribs in a ceramic baking dish and pour over the Smoky Chili BBQ Sauce. Make sure the ribs are covered in the marinade. Cover and refrigerate overnight to let the marinade flavors soak in.

After this time, remove the ribs from the fridge and let them come to room temperature.

Preheat the oven to 300°F (150°C) Gas 2.

Stir the marinade and spoon over the ribs. Cover the dish with foil and cook in the preheated oven for 2½ hours.

Remove the ribs from the oven and take off the foil. Baste the ribs with the sauce, then return to the oven for a further 1 hour.

Remove from the oven, cover, and set aside to rest for 15 minutes.

Cut up the ribs and serve on large platter. Eat with your hands!

2 racks baby back pork ribs

**1 recipe of Smoky Chili BBQ Sauce
(see page 12)**

SERVES 4—6

Hogwild BOURBON
PORK CHOPS
with APPLES

This is definitely a dish for bourbon lovers. The pork chops are marinated overnight in a Hogwild Bourbon Glaze, then cooked in a smoking hot cast iron pan with apples. I absolutely love this dish as it soaks up everything great about the South: pork, bourbon, honey, and molasses.

Rinse the pork chops in cold water and pat dry with a paper towel. Put the chops in a ceramic baking dish and pour over the Hogwild Bourbon Glaze. Cover and put in the fridge for 8–24 hours to let the marinade flavors soak in.

After this time, remove the marinated pork from the fridge and let it come to room temperature.

Heat a large cast iron pan over a medium–high heat until just smoking. Remove the chops from the marinade, place in the hot pan, and reduce the heat to medium. Brown the chops for 3–5 minutes per side.

Meanwhile, pour the remaining glaze into a separate saucepan and bring to a boil. Reduce the heat and simmer the glaze until reduced by half.

Once the chops have browned, add the apple slices to the pan with the pork and turn down the heat. Pour over the reduced glaze and cover. Cook for a further 5 minutes, or to the desired doneness.

COOK'S NOTE: Due to the high alcohol and sugar content of the glaze, if you are cooking over gas the glaze may ignite into a small flame. Don't be alarmed, just let the alcohol burn off and the flame will die out—it only takes a few minutes.

4 center-cut pork chops, bone in

1 recipe of Hogwild Bourbon Glaze, (see page 13)

2 Granny Smith apples, cored and sliced into wedges

SERVES 4

Fermented BLACK BEAN SPICY PASTE

⅓ cup/45 g Chinese fermented black beans

2 small Thai chiles, finely chopped

1 garlic clove, finely chopped

1 tablespoon freshly grated ginger

2 tablespoons toasted sesame oil

¼ cup/4 tablespoons kecap manis (Indonesian soy sauce)

YIELDS ½ CUP/120 ML

Fermented black beans are used extensively in Asian cooking and give a deep salty flavor to any dish. They taste great and look even better. Add them to a dipping sauce or blend in a marinade. You won't be disappointed.

Put all the ingredients in a bowl and mix together.

Store the paste in an airtight container in the fridge for up to 2 weeks, or you can also freeze it for up to 6 months.

To use, put the pork in a ceramic dish, pour over the paste, and rub it into the meat. Leave to marinate for 8–24 hours in the fridge. Let the meat come to room temperature, then cook according to the recipe on page 20, or as preferred. This paste can also be used on chicken, beef, and shrimp/prawns.

Cajun SPICE RUB

2 teaspoons ground cumin

2 teaspoons cayenne pepper

2 tablespoons Spanish smoked paprika (pimentòn)

2 teaspoons dried thyme

2 teaspoons dried oregano

1 teaspoon dried garlic powder

2 teaspoons turbinado/demerara sugar

1 teaspoon sea salt

1 teaspoon ground black pepper

YIELDS SCANT ½ CUP/
6½ TABLESPOONS

Cajun spices are a wonderful addition to any kind of meat, fish, or poultry. When cooked, they blacken and take on a wonderful spicy, earthy flavor. Sometimes I add a pinch of this spice mix to mixed nuts sautéed in olive oil for a snack or to serve with a glass of wine when friends pop by.

Put all the ingredients in a bowl and mix together.

Store the rub in a glass jar with a tight-fitting lid for up to 6 months.

To use, put the pork in a ceramic dish, sprinkle over the spice rub, and rub it into the meat. Leave to marinate for 8–24 hours in the fridge. Let the meat come to room temperature, then cook according to the recipe on page 23, or as preferred. This rub can also be used on fish, chicken, and turkey.

Szechuan RUB

1 tablespoon Szechaun peppercorns

1 tablespoon dried chili flakes

1 teaspoon chili powder

1 teaspoon dried garlic powder

1 teaspoon ground ginger

1 teaspoon coarse sea salt

1 teaspoon black peppercorns

YIELDS SCANT ¼ CUP/
3½ TABLESPOONS

The Chinese province of Szechuan is known for cooking with fiery chiles and salty condiments. Wonderful dishes come out of this area and this simple rub is perfect to keep on hand.

Put all the ingredients into an electric spice grinder and process to a coarse powder.

Store the rub in a glass jar with a tight-fitting lid for up to 6 months.

To use, put the pork in a ceramic dish, sprinkle over the spice rub, and rub it into the meat. Leave to marinate for 8–24 hours in the fridge. Let the meat come to room temperature, then cook as preferred. This rub can also be used on chicken, beef, and lamb.

Fennel Anise SALT RUB

2 tablespoons fennel seeds

1 tablespoon anise seeds

1 tablespoon fennel pollen

1 teaspoon dried ground orange peel

1 teaspoon Fleur de Sel salt

½ teaspoon ground black pepper

YIELDS SCANT ⅓ CUP/
5 TABLESPOONS

This rub is packed with fennel liquorish flavors and adding fennel pollen, too, really kicks it up a notch. If you are lucky enough to have fennel growing nearby, make your own pollen, it's so easy to do.

In a frying pan set over a high heat, roast the fennel and anise seeds for 2–3 minutes, stirring continuously so they don't burn. Pour the roasted seeds into an electric spice grinder and add the fennel pollen, ground orange peel, salt, and pepper. Grind until you have a coarse powder.

Store the rub in a glass jar with a tight-fitting lid for up to 6 months.

To use, put the pork in a ceramic dish, sprinkle over the spice rub, and rub it into the meat. Leave to marinate for 8–24 hours in the fridge. Let the meat come to room temperature, then cook as preferred. This rub can also be used on poultry, fish, and beef.

COOK'S NOTE: To make your own fennel pollen, put the fresh flowers in a paper bag and leave in a cool place to dry for about 2 weeks. Shake the bag vigorously to dislodge the pollen, then remove the stems from the bag. Store the pollen in a glass jar for up to 6 months.

Fermented BLACK BEAN
PORK TENDERLOINS
with PEACHES

Let your eyes feast on this beautiful dish of ripe peaches with dark fermented black beans. Of course, summer is the best time for peaches, but don't be put off if you want to make it any other time—just select a seasonal fruit that will compliment the pork and the saltiness of the beans.

Wash the pork under cold water and pat dry with a paper towel. Put the pork tenderloins in a ceramic baking dish, pour over the Fermented Black Bean Spicy Paste and rub into the pork. Cover and refrigerate for 6–24 hours.

After this time, remove the marinated pork from the fridge and let it come to room temperature.

Preheat the oven to 375°F (190°C) Gas 5.

Cut the peaches into quarters and place them in a glass or ceramic bowl. Pour over the honey and toss to coat. Set aside.

Heat an ovenproof sauté pan over a medium–high heat. Remove the pork from the marinade and shake off any excess sauce. Drizzle the pan with a little vegetable oil and sear the tenderloins on all sides.

Pour the remaining marinade into the pan and arrange the peaches around the pork. Transfer the pan to the preheated oven and roast the pork for 15–20 minutes. When done, remove from the oven, cover, and leave to rest for 10 minutes.

Slice the pork crosswise and serve in bowls with the sauce and peaches, and wedges of fresh lime.

COOK'S NOTE: Black Forbidden Rice is delicious with this dish.

2 pork tenderloins (weighing about 1½ lb./680 g in total)

1 recipe of Fermented Black Bean Spicy Paste (see page 18)

4 ripe peaches

2 tablespoons orange blossom honey

vegetable oil, for searing

4 limes, quartered, to serve

SERVES 4–6

Cajun CRISPY
PORK BELLY
with KUMQUAT *dipping sauce*

There is nothing in the world better than crispy pork belly. The combination of earthy Cajun spices and the citrus of kumquats is light and bright. This is perfect as an appetizer on tossed salad greens or served on rice for a heartier course

Rinse the pork belly under cold water and pat dry with a paper towel. Put the pork in a lidded pan and add the bay leaves, white wine, salt, and peppercorns. Pour in enough cold water to cover the pork by 2 inches/ 5 cm. Cover and bring to a boil over a medium–high heat, then reduce the heat and let the pork simmer for 1½ hours.

To make the kumquat dipping sauce, whisk all the ingredients together in a bowl, cover, and put in the fridge until ready to use.

Remove the pork from the pan and place on large plate. Let it rest for 10 minutes, allowing it to cool enough to handle, then sprinkle the Cajun Spice Rub over the pork and rub it in.

Slice the pork into 1½-inch/4-cm slices. Heat a cast iron pan over a high heat until just smoking. Add a splash of vegetable oil, not too much, and sear the pork slices for 2 minutes on each side. Turn down the heat to medium–low and continue to cook for a further 4 minutes, until crispy. The Cajun spices will blacken the pork.

Serve the pork with the cold dipping sauce.

2 lb./900 g pork belly, skin removed

2 bay leaves

¼ cup/60 ml white wine

1 teaspoon sea salt

1 teaspoon black peppercorns

4 teaspoons Cajun Spice Rub (see page 18)

vegetable oil, for searing

KUMQUAT DIPPING SAUCE

6 kumquats, finely sliced (discard any seeds)

½ red Serrano chile, finely sliced

½ cup/120 ml cider vinegar

2 tablespoons honey

1 teaspoon mirin (Japanese rice wine)

SERVES 4–6

Juniper Berry BRINE

1 tablespoon juniper berries

4 garlic cloves, peeled

4 fresh bay leaves

1 sprig rosemary

1 cup/130 g Kosher/table salt

1 cup/240 ml white wine

YIELDS 9 CUPS/2.2 LITRES

This is when to get out the mortar and pestle and bruise the juniper berries to let those fantastic floral aromas jump out at you. This brine works well with any cut of pork and the flavors soak deep down into the meat.

In a mortar and pestle, pound the juniper berries, garlic, and bay leaves until they are smashed.

Put the juniper berries, garlic, and bay into a large pan with all the other ingredients, add 2 quarts/litres water, and set over a medium–high heat. Bring to a boil and stir until all the salt has dissolved. Remove from the heat and let cool completely before using.

To use, put the meat in a large pan and pour over the brine, making sure the meat is submerged (add more cold water if needed). Cover and put in the fridge overnight, then rinse the meat and cook according to the recipe on page 26, or as preferred.

COOK'S NOTE: If you need to get the brine cooled fast, pour the hot brine into a bowl and place the bowl in an ice bath.

Anise and APPLE CIDER BRINE

1 tablespoon anise seeds

½ cup/120 ml (hard) apple cider

½ cup/65 g Kosher/table salt

2 garlic cloves, bashed

1 tablespoon black peppercorns

4 fresh bay leaves

YIELDS 9 CUPS/2.2 LITRES

Apple cider gives this brine a kick. If possible, use unfiltered cider as it does make a difference. I tend to use this brine solely for pork as the apple flavors go together so well. The addition of the anise just adds a little surprise.

Put all the ingredients in a large pan and add 2 quarts/litres water. Set the pan over a medium–high heat and bring to a boil, stirring until all the salt has dissolved. Remove from the heat and let cool completely before using.

To use, put the meat in a large pan and pour over the brine, making sure the meat is submerged (add more cold water if needed). Cover and put in the fridge overnight, then rinse the meat and cook according to the recipe on page 29, or as preferred.

Blackberry and SAGE GLAZE

1½ lb./680 g blackberries, washed

¼ cup/60 ml cassis liqueur

1 cup/200 g dark brown sugar

2 tablespoons finely chopped fresh sage

freshly squeezed juice of 1 lemon

YIELDS SCANT 1½ CUPS/360 ML

Two earthy and strong flavors come together here to create a sweet, tangy glaze—not too sweet, and with a little sourness in there to surprise you. I created this recipe to glaze ham, but it's also perfect for pork chops or even served alongside grilled lamb. Either way, make the most of blackberry season.

Put all the ingredients in a saucepan set over a medium–high heat, stir, and bring to a boil. Turn down the heat and simmer, as if making jam, for 40 minutes, stirring occasionally. Remove from the heat and let cool completely before using or storing.

Store the glaze in an airtight container in the fridge for up to 1 month.

Use according to the recipe on page 26 to marinate pork, lamb, or turkey, or simply serve alongside roast meats.

Blackberry AND SAGE
GLAZED HAM

a 5½-lb./2-kg boneless whole ham

1 recipe of Juniper Berry Brine
(see page 24)

1 tablespoon whole cloves, crushed

1 recipe of Blackberry and Sage Glaze
(see page 25)

cracked black pepper

a Dutch oven/large lidded casserole

a roasting pan with a rack

a meat thermometer

SERVES 4—6

This recipe came about when my local butcher, Nathan, called to say he had just taken delivery of a whole Berkshire pig from a local farmer and there was a ham to be had. Then a neighbor dropped by with a haul of freshly picked blackberries. So with a fresh ham and a bowl spilling over with berries I got to work straight away, and what a treat it was.

Rinse the ham under cold water. Put in a Dutch oven or casserole and pour over the Juniper Berry Brine, making sure the ham is submerged. Add more cold water if needed. Place a plate or a small pan lid on top of the ham to keep it submerged in the brine. Cover and put in the fridge overnight.

Preheat the oven to 350°F (180°C) Gas 4.

Remove the ham from the fridge and rinse under cold water. Put the ham on a rack set in a roasting pan. Score the fat, sprinkle with the crushed cloves, and season with cracked black pepper.

Pour 2 cups/480 ml water into the roasting pan, then put the ham in the preheated oven. Cook for 1 hour, then reduce the oven temperature to 300°F (150°C) Gas 2 and cook for a further 30 minutes. Whilst roasting, check occasionally that the water in the base of the pan hasn't dried out and replenish when needed.

Remove the ham from the oven and spoon over the Blackberry and Sage Glaze. Return the ham to the oven and cook for a further 30 minutes or until a meat thermometer inserted into the center of the ham reads 145°F (63°C).

Remove the ham from the oven and loosely cover with foil. Allow the ham to rest for 20 minutes, then cut into thick slices and serve.

Roasted BACON-WRAPPED
PORK LOIN
with PRUNE stuffing

I like to make this roast for a dinner party. It's so simple to put together and it's perfect with just a simple side. Slow roasted, it allows the flavors of the stuffing to infuse the meat along with the apple juices. The smoky bacon helps keep the meat moist and lends a subtle smokiness all around. Ask your butcher to butterfly the loin for you.

Put the pork loin in a large bowl and pour over the Anise and Apple Cider Brine, making sure the meat is submerged. Cover and put in the fridge for 8–24 hours.

Put the prunes for the stuffing in a bowl and cover with water. Leave to soak overnight.

To make the stuffing, heat a frying pan over a medium heat. Add the olive oil, garlic, and shallots and cook until golden, then add the prunes, thyme, parsley, and breadcrumbs and stir together. Season and continue to cook for 5 minutes. Remove from the heat and set aside to cool completely. (This can be done the day before and stored in the fridge overnight.)

Preheat the oven to 375°F (190°C) Gas 5.

Remove the pork from the fridge and drain off the brine, then rinse the loin and pat dry. Lay a piece of plastic wrap/clingfilm on a surface and lay the bacon strips in a row next to each other. Put the pork on top with the butterfly side facing up. Spread the cooled stuffing over the pork and use the plastic wrap/clingfilm to help roll it up. Remove the wrap/film and tie with kitchen twine. Put the rolled pork in a baking dish and pour in the apple juice. Season with salt and pepper, scatter over the thyme sprigs, and drizzle with olive oil. Roast in the preheated oven for 15 minutes, then reduce the heat to 325°F (160°C) Gas 3 and cook for a further 1 hour.

Remove from the oven, cover loosely with foil, and let rest for 15 minutes, then carve into thick slices and serve.

2½-lb./1.2-kg pork loin roast, butterflied

1 recipe of Anise and Apple Cider Brine (see page 24)

4 thick slices apple-smoked bacon

½ cup/120 ml apple juice or cider

a few fresh thyme sprigs

olive oil, for drizzling

sea salt and cracked black pepper

STUFFING

1 cup/135 g dried prunes, roughly chopped

2 tablespoons olive oil

1 garlic clove, finely chopped

2 shallots, finely diced

1 tablespoon fresh thyme leaves

a small bunch of fresh flat-leaf parsley, chopped

1 cup/80 g toasted breadcrumbs

sea salt and cracked black pepper

kitchen twine

SERVES 4—6

BEEF

You will have a lot of fun with the recipes in this chapter. Bursting with flavor and color, cooking with these spices, marinades, flavored oils, and butters, beef may never be the same.

As with all meats, buy beef that is local, organic, and sustainable wherever possible. Animals that have lived free of stress make for good meat. Grass-fed beef is more readily available and you will find it at your local market—the taste is unbelievable.

Beef needs to be seasoned before cooking, there is no way around it—even the best steaks need salt and pepper to bring out the flavors, otherwise they will be bland. Big bold rubs, like the Coffee & Chili Rub, season the meat with warm spices and the surprise of coffee adds a pleasing layer of flavor. Enjoy the wonderful smoky salt in the Smoky African Rub and the dried herbs of the Prairie Rub: these all intensify the flavor of the meat.

A good tip when grilling meat is to tie a bunch of herbs, such as rosemary, thyme, and oregano, together with twine to make a herbal brush. Use this to dip into marinades and flavored oils and baste the meat as it cooks. Throw herbs and citrus leaves onto the hot coals—they add flavor and smell divine.

Steaks on the barbecue are not just for the summer months. You can easily cook them in a cast iron grill pan on the stove top when the weather turns cooler and enjoy the rubs and butters all year round.

I like to make up batches of flavored butters and then keep them in the freezer to use as I want. This works really well for some seasonal produce, especially truffles. In the summer, you can melt wonderfully earthy winter truffle butter over barbecued charred ears of corn. Dollop flavored butters on top of meats or fish straight off the grill and generously spread over grilled breads.

Matambre was the jewel for me in this chapter. I had heard about it for years from my Argentinian brother-in-law, Eduardo. After every trip to Buenos Aires, my sister Elvena would remind me about it, and urge me to make it. Everyone will love the look of it—when you slice into it you see the swirl of color from the chard, peppers and, of course, a bright yellow egg in the middle, just like a Swiss roll. Finally, I made it and she is absolutely right of course! I love it. Serve thick slices with a big bowl of Chimichurri.

When preparing beef, especially when you have seasoned it and placed it in the refrigerator to marinade, bring the meat to room temperature before cooking. Once you have finished cooking, cover the meat with foil and allow to rest for at least 10–20 minutes before serving.

The simplest of seasonings are fun, too, such as finishing salts, spices, and fresh herbs. Sprinkle lemon salt or a good pinch of sumac at the end, just before serving. Or tear a handful of fresh parsley leaves, toss in a little oil and lemon juice and top on a finished steak or piece of meat. The most rustic ways to add flavor can be the best and the easiest if you don't have time to mix up a rub or marinade.

Matambre MARINADE

1 teaspoon dried thyme

1 teaspoon dried oregano

1 teaspoon dried marjoram

1 teaspoon sea salt

½ teaspoon dried chili flakes

2 garlic cloves, finely chopped

¼ cup/60 ml red wine vinegar

¼ cup/60 ml olive oil

YIELDS SCANT ¾ CUP/150 ML

In Argentina they eat a lot of good beef, which is always seasoned before cooking. You could keep this as a dry spice rub, substituting dried garlic powder for the garlic cloves and without adding the olive oil or vinegar, but I like to marinade steaks in this herbed oil.

Put all the ingredients in a bowl and mix together.

Store the marinade in an airtight container in the fridge for up to 2 weeks.

To use, put the meat in a ceramic dish, pour over the marinade, and leave to marinate for 8–24 hours in the fridge. Let the meat come to room temperature, then cook according to the recipe on page 36, or as preferred.

Coffee and CHILE RUB

2 tablespoons finely ground coffee

1 tablespoon chipotle chili powder

1 teaspoon ground cumin

1 teaspoon Spanish smoked paprika (pimentòn)

½ teaspoon sea salt

¼ teaspoon ground black pepper

YIELDS SCANT ¼ CUP/
4 TABLESPOONS

You wouldn't think that coffee could be used in savory foods as a seasoning, but prepare to be surprised as it gives a whole other flavor and depth to dishes. You can use coffee granules, instant coffee, or a cup of coffee to enhance pieces of meat.

Put all the ingredients in a bowl and mix together.

Store the rub in a glass jar with a tight-fitting lid for up to 1 month.

To use, put the meat in a ceramic dish, sprinkle over the rub and rub it into the meat. Leave to marinate for 8–24 hours in the fridge. Let the meat come to room temperature, then cook according to the recipe on page 39, or as preferred. This rub can also be used on pork.

Korean MARINADE

⅓ cup/80 ml vegetable oil

⅓ cup/80 ml soy sauce

¼ cup/60 ml toasted sesame oil

3 tablespoons sherry

4 tablespoons brown sugar

3 tablespoons curry powder

2 tablespoons grated fresh ginger

4 garlic cloves, peeled and bashed

3 scallions/spring onions, roughly chopped

sea salt and cracked black pepper

YIELDS 1½ CUPS/360 ML

This is one of those marinades I make over and over again and never tire of. It's inspired of my love of Korean food and grilling combined. Use it on ribs and fire up the grill.

Put all the ingredients except for the salt and pepper in a blender or food processor and process until blended, then season with salt and pepper.

Store the marinade in an airtight container in the fridge for up to 10 days.

To use, put the meat in a ceramic dish, pour over the marinade and leave to marinate for 8–24 hours in the fridge. Let the meat come to room temperature, then cook as preferred. This marinade can also be used on pork, tofu and lamb.

MATAMBRE

My brother-in-law, Eduardo, is Argentinian and one of his favorite things to eat when he visits Buenos Aires is Matambre, which translated means "Hunger Killer". It's served as an appetizer or can be eaten in a bread roll. His sister makes it especially for him and this is my version of their family recipe.

a 2-lb./900-g flank steak

1 recipe of Matambre Marinade
(see page 34)

6 leafy stalks red Swiss chard

⅓ cup/30 g grated Parmesan cheese

2 garlic cloves, finely chopped

½ cup/60 g Kalamata olives,
pitted and roughly chopped

a small bunch of fresh flat-leaf parsley
leaves, roughly chopped

a small bunch of fresh marjoram leaves,
roughly chopped

a small bunch of fresh oregano leaves,
roughly chopped

2 roasted red bell peppers

6 hard-boiled eggs, peeled

6 fresh bay leaves

olive oil, to drizzle

sea salt and cracked black pepper

1 recipe of Chimichurri (see page 41),
to serve

kitchen twine

SERVES 6–8

Rinse the steak under cold water and pat dry with a paper towel. Put the meat between 2 pieces of plastic wrap/clingfilm and, using a mallet, pound the meat until it is paper thin, being careful not to tear it. Remove the plastic wrap/clingfilm and place the steak in a ceramic dish. Pour over the Matambre Marinade and refrigerate for 6–24 hours.

Preheat the oven to 375°F (190°C) Gas 5. Remove the steak from the fridge and lay out on a large piece of plastic wrap/clingfilm.

Finely julienne the chard and put in a mixing bowl. Add the Parmesan, garlic, olives, parsley, marjoram, and oregano and mix together. Season with salt and pepper to taste.

Spread the chard mixture evenly over the steak until you have completely covered it, then layer the peppers on top. Lay the boiled eggs in a row down the center of the steak.

Taking the side of the steak nearest to you, roll up the meat like a cigar. Tie securely with kitchen twine at even intervals along the steak, making sure you tuck the end in. Place in a roasting pan and slip the bay leaves under the twine. Season generously, with salt and pepper, then drizzle with olive oil.

Cook in the preheated oven for 1 hour, then remove from the oven. Cover loosely with foil and allow to rest for 20 minutes.

Slice thick and serve hot with Chimichurri. You can also refrigerate and eat cold with a salad or in a sandwich.

Coffee AND CHILE
SHORT RIBS

I discovered on a recent trip to the Southwest that they don't just drink coffee or use it for the odd tiramisù, rather brine, marinade, rub and barbecue with it. Whether it's a strong espresso or a mild cup of Joe, it's used to give an earthy layer to big bold meats, especially pork and beef.

Put the ribs in a bowl and sprinkle with the Coffee and Chile Rub. Mix together ensuring the ribs are well coated. Cover and refrigerate for 6–24 hours.

After this time, remove the ribs from the fridge and let them come to room temperature.

Preheat the oven to 350°F (180°C) Gas 4.

In a Dutch oven or casserole large enough to fit the ribs, heat the oil over a medium–high heat. Working in batches, brown the ribs on all sides for about 8–10 minutes per batch. Remove all the ribs from the pan and set aside on a plate.

Add the garlic, onion, and Jalapeños to the hot pan and brown. Pour in the coffee, chopped tomatoes, and vinegar and bring to a simmer. Put the ribs back in the pan and put the lid on. Transfer the pan to the preheated oven and cook the ribs for 3 hours until tender.

Remove from the oven and rest for 30 minutes. Sprinkle with torn basil leaves and serve in bowls with lots of sauce.

4 lb./1.8 kg beef short ribs cut into squares between the bones (about 2½ x 2½ inches/7 x 7 cm)

1 recipe of Coffee and Chile Rub (see page 35)

3 tablespoons olive oil

4 garlic cloves, finely chopped

1 yellow onion, roughly chopped

2 Jalapeño chiles, roughly chopped

1 cup/240 ml freshly brewed espresso

1 x 28 oz. can/2 x 400 g cans chopped tomatoes

2 tablespoons balsamic vinegar

sea salt and cracked black pepper

torn basil leaves, to garnish

a Dutch oven/large lidded casserole

SERVES 4–6

Sloppy Joe SPICE MIX

2 teaspoons smoked paprika

2 teaspoons chili powder

1 teaspoon celery seeds

1 teaspoon dried garlic powder

1 teaspoon dried oregano

1 teaspoon English mustard powder

½ teaspoon sea salt

1 teaspoon ground black pepper

YIELDS SCANT ¼ CUP/
3½ TABLESPOONS

This spice mix is only for a Sloppy Joe. It is a little bit of everything and a bit more detailed than most Joes. I have asked all my friends exactly what goes in a Sloppy Joe sandwich that makes them so good and nobody seems quite able to put their finger on it. It's all in their childhood memories.

Put all the ingredients in a bowl and mix together.

Store the spice mix in a glass jar with a tight-fitting lid for up to 3 months.

Use according to the recipe on page 42.

Prairie RUB

1 teaspoon sea salt

1 teaspoon ground black pepper

2 teaspoons mustard powder

1 teaspoon Spanish paprika

1 tablespoon dried sage

1 tablespoon dried oregano

1 tablespoon dried rosemary

1 tablespoon dried thyme

1 teaspoon dried garlic powder

YIELDS ⅓ CUP/
6 TABLESPOONS

This spice mix came about when I was cooking a large Porterhouse steak for a party. I needed a fun name to call it and decided that "Prairie Rub" would have a romantic olden day feel to it. Apart from that, it's a stand up spice mix that works really well with large pieces of beef.

Put all the ingredients in a bowl and mix together.

Store the rub in a glass jar with a tight-fitting lid for up to 6 months.

To use, put the meat in a ceramic dish, sprinkle over the rub and rub it into the meat. Leave to marinate for 8–24 hours in the fridge. Let the meat come to room temperature, then cook according to the recipe on page 44, or as preferred. This rub can also be used on pork and chicken.

Sofrito with SMOKED PIMENTÒN

¼ cup/60 ml olive oil

2 large yellow onions, finely chopped

2 garlic cloves, finely chopped

2 lb./900 g (about 12) ripe tomatoes, roughly chopped

1 fresh bay leaf

½ teaspoon Spanish smoked paprika (pimentòn)

½ cup/120 ml Madeira wine

sea salt and cracked black pepper

YIELDS SCANT 2 CUPS/450 ML

Every culture has a version of this recipe. Sofrito is a tomato, garlic, and onion-based paste, which can be used in soups, stews, paellas, or as a base for pizzas. It's versatile and friendly and I highly recommend you keep a jar handy in the fridge. Jazz it up by adding chiles, bell peppers, and wines to this basic recipe.

Heat a cast iron pan over a medium–high heat and add the oil, onions, and garlic. Sauté until soft and golden brown, stirring frequently.

Add the tomatoes, bay leaf, and pimentòn, stir, and continue to cook for a further 5 minutes. Pour in the Madeira wine and season with salt and pepper. Stir and cook for about 10 minutes, until the mixture becomes a thick sauce. Remove from the heat and leave to cool.

Store the sofrito in an airtight container in the fridge for up to 1 month.

The sofrito can be used with pork or chicken as well as beef, stirred into pasta and soups, or on pizzas.

ChimiCHURRI

a small bunch of fresh oregano leaves

a small bunch of fresh marjoram leaves

a bunch of fresh flat-leaf parsley leaves

1 small red Jalapeño chile, finely chopped

2 garlic cloves, finely chopped

½ cup/120 ml red wine vinegar

1 cup/240 ml extra virgin olive oil

cracked black pepper

YIELDS SCANT 2 CUPS/450 ML

This wonderful herbed sauce is from Argentina and the gauchos make it to go with their meats. I use a lot of fresh herbs in my cooking, so this really is one of my favorites. I love to dip a freshly torn baguette into it, use it as a salad dressing, or drizzle over grilled meats.

Put the oregano, marjoram, and parsley on a wooden board and finely chop. Put the Jalapeño and garlic in a ceramic bowl along with the chopped herbs. Pour in the red wine vinegar and olive oil, stir well, and season to taste with salt and pepper.

Cover and leave in the fridge until ready to use, so the flavors can mingle, then bring to room temperature when ready to serve.

Old FASHIONED
SLOPPY JOES

2 tablespoons olive oil

2 garlic cloves, finely chopped

1 yellow onion, diced

1 celery stalk, finely sliced

1 red bell pepper, finely diced

1 lb./450 g ground/minced beef chuck

1 recipe of Sloppy Joe Spice Mix
(see page 40)

2 tablespoons tomato paste/purée

2 tablespoons Worcestershire sauce

1 x 28-oz. can/2 x 400-g cans chopped
tomatoes

sea salt and cracked black pepper

TO SERVE

4 ciabatta rolls

a drizzle of olive oil

thin slices of red onion (optional)

pickles (optional)

a Dutch oven/large lidded casserole

SERVES 6

I know I am calling this "old fashioned", but I wanted to put a spin on this childhood classic. Instead of the usual burger bun, I toast ciabatta rolls drizzled with good olive oil, then serve them up with pickles. It seems everyone has a Sloppy Joe memory, so make them for a weekend treat and hear everyone's childhood stories.

Set a Dutch oven/casserole over a medium–high heat. Add the oil, garlic, and onion and sauté for about 3–5 minutes, until tender and golden brown. Add the celery and pepper and continue to cook for a further 5 minutes until they have taken on some color.

Add the beef and Sloppy Joe Spice Mix and cook for about 6–8 minutes, until browned, stirring frequently and breaking up any larger pieces.

Stir in the tomato paste/purée, Worcestershire sauce, and chopped tomatoes and stir to combine. Season with salt and pepper, then cover the pan and reduce the heat to medium–low. Continue to simmer for 30 minutes, stirring occasionally to avoid the mixture sticking to the pan.

Cut the ciabatta rolls in half. Drizzle with the olive oil and grill until golden brown.

Top the bottom half of the ciabatta rolls with generous spoonfuls of the Sloppy Joe meat. Allow the juices to soak into the bread. Garnish with sliced red onions, if using, then top with the remaining half of ciabatta. Serve with pickles, if you wish.

Prairie RUBBED
PORTERHOUSE STEAK
with CHIMICHURRI

Wow your guests by serving this steak straight off the grill and carving it at the table. Rubbed with a wonderful array of earthy herbs that will remind you of the Prairie, you will find you'll be grilling this again and again. It's a great steak for sharing.

Wash the steak and pat dry with a paper towel. Drizzle with olive oil and sprinkle the steak on both sides with the Prairie Rub. Season with salt and pepper, cover, and refrigerate for 6–24 hours.

After this time, remove the steak from the fridge and let it come to room temperature.

Heat a grill/barbecue to medium–high. Place the steak on the grill/barbecue and cook for 8–10 minutes on each side for rare and continue to cook if you prefer medium to well done.

Remove the steak form the grill, cover, and let it rest for 10 minutes.

Carve and serve with the Chimichurri sauce.

1 large Porterhouse steak,
2 inches/5 cm thick

2 tablespoons olive oil

3 tablespoons Prairie Rub (see page 40)

sea salt and cracked black pepper

1 recipe of Chimichurri (see page 41),
to serve

SERVES 4

Smoky African RUB

1 teaspoon smoked sea salt

1 teaspoon coarse-ground garlic powder

1 teaspoon ground black pepper

1 tablespoon dried chili flakes

1 teaspoon fenugreek seeds

2 dried bay leaves

YIELDS 3 TABLESPOONS

When I lived in Cape Town, the weekend pastime was to light a *braai*, which is the Afrikaans word for barbecue. Perhaps not so much a pastime as a way of life, everyone has a lot of fun cooking up a storm with recipes handed down through families. This is a simple rub, which is laced with smoked salt, giving a hearty bite.

Put all the ingredients into an electric spice grinder and process to a coarse powder.

Store the spice mix in a glass jar with a tight-fitting lid for up to 6 months.

To use, put the meat in a ceramic dish, sprinkle over the rub, and rub it into the meat. Leave to marinate for 8–24 hours in the fridge. Let the meat come to room temperature, then cook according to the recipe on page 48, or as preferred. This rub can also be used on pork and poultry.

Cowboy CHILI SPICES

2 tablespoons ancho chili powder

2 teaspoons ground cumin

1 teaspoon smoked paprika

1 teaspoon ground cinnamon

1 tablespoon chipotle chiles in adobe sauce, chopped

sea salt and cracked black pepper

YIELDS ¼ CUP/4 TABLESPOONS

The thing about seasonings is that they really are a matter of taste, especially when it comes to chili. I eat a lot of spicy foods and love cooking with chiles and spices. Although this is not a fiery hot chili, feel free to experiment and change this up by adding more chiles or taking some out.

Put all the ingredients in a bowl and stir well to mix. Season with salt and pepper.

Store the paste in an airtight container in the fridge for up to 10 days.

Use according to the recipe on page 51, or rub into beef, lamb or poultry and leave to marinate for 8–24 hours in the fridge. Let the meat come to room temperature, then cook as preferred.

Roasted JALAPEÑO BUTTER

3 green Jalapeño chiles

2 sticks/225 g unsalted butter, at room temperature

sea salt and cracked black pepper

YIELDS 1 CUP/240 G

Grilling or roasting the Jalapeños over a gas flame imparts a sweet smoky flavor but still leaves the spice. Store the butter in the freezer, then cut slices to melt on hot grilled corn or butter a toasted burger bun to add spice.

Roast the Jalapeños on a grill/barbecue or gas stove top until the skins are blackened. Set aside on a board to cool.

When cool, peel off the skins and roughly chop the Jalapeños. Put the chiles and butter in a food processor and process until smooth. Season with salt and pepper and refrigerate until ready to use.

To make a butter roll, spoon the butter mixture onto a piece of plastic wrap/clingfilm. Fold the wrap/film over the butter and roll into a sausage shape. Twist the ends to secure and store in the fridge or freezer. When you're ready to use the butter, slice off discs as desired.

To use, melt over grilled meats and vegetables or serve with fresh breads or cornbread.

Smoked SEA SALT BUTTER

2½ teaspoons smoked sea salt

2 sticks/225 g unsalted butter, at room temperature

cracked black pepper

YIELDS 1 CUP/240 G

This is a robust butter, salty and smoky, which lends itself perfectly to grilled meats and vegetables. Spoon some through rice or potatoes just before serving to pack in flavor. Smoked salts are easy to find in your local supermarket.

Put the salt and butter in a food processor and process until smooth. Season with pepper and refrigerate until ready to use.

To make a butter roll, spoon the butter mixture onto a piece of plastic wrap/clingfilm. Fold the wrap/film over the butter and roll into a sausage shape. Twist the ends to secure and store in the fridge or freezer. When you're ready to use the butter, slice off discs as desired.

To use, melt over grilled meats and vegetables or serve with fresh bread.

African RUBBED
GRILLED SKIRT STEAK
with SMOKED BUTTER

Skirt steak is a forgotten treasure. It is full of flavor and the perfect cut of meat to marinate or rub with spices. It is best eaten straight off the grill, sandwiched in a baguette lavishly spread with smoked butter and topped with watercress. The heat of the steak melts the butter in a gooey piece of bliss.

Rinse the skirt steak under cold water and pat dry with a paper towel. Put in a ceramic dish and drizzle with a little olive oil. Sprinkle the Smoky African Rub over both sides of the steak. Season with cracked black pepper, then cover and refrigerate overnight.

After this time, remove the steak from the fridge and let it come to room temperature.

Heat a grill/barbecue to high. Put the steak on the grill/barbecue and cook for 4–5 minutes on each side. If you prefer your steak well done, continue to cook for a few more minutes.

Cut the baguette in half and toast on the grill, then spread with some of the Smoked Sea Salt Butter. Lay the steak on the bottom half of the baguette, sprinkle over the watercress sprigs, and top with the lid. Cut into thick slices and serve.

1 lb./450 g skirt steak

olive oil, to drizzle

1 recipe of Smoky African Rub
(see page 46)

cracked black pepper, to season

TO SERVE

a rustic baguette

Smoked Sea Salt Butter (see page 47)

2 cups/100 g watercress sprigs

SERVES 4–6

Cowboy CHILI

This is a great party dish. Have lots of bowls with toppings of crème fraîche, cilantro/coriander, lime wedges, and cheese. This is delicious served with cornbread spread with Roasted Jalapeño Butter (see page 47).

Wash the meat under cold water and pat dry with a paper towel. Cut the beef into 1-inch/2.5-cm pieces and put in a bowl.

Add 2 tablespoons of the olive oil to the Cowboy Chili Spices paste and stir, then add the paste to the beef and mix well until evenly coated. Cover the meat and refrigerate for 8–24 hours to allow the flavors to meld.

Once the beef has marinated, put the remaining 2 tablespoons of oil in a Dutch oven/large casserole set over medium heat. Add the garlic, onion, and chiles and sauté for about 5 minutes, until tender and golden brown. Add the seasoned beef and cook for about 6–8 minutes, until browned, stirring frequently so as not to stick to the pan.

Add the bay leaf, wine, tomato paste/purée, and chopped tomatoes to the pan and stir. Bring to a boil then lower the heat, cover with a lid, and simmer gently for 45 minutes, stirring occasionally.

Add the black beans and chocolate to the pan and stir. Replace the lid and cook for a further 15 minutes.

Spoon the chili into bowls and garnish with crème fraîche and fresh cilantro/coriander. Serve with lime wedges on the side for squeezing.

2 lb./900 g best chuck beef

1 recipe of Cowboy Chili Spices (see page 46)

4 tablespoons olive oil

2 garlic cloves, finely chopped

1 red onion, diced

2 Jalapeño chiles, thinly sliced

1 bay leaf

2 cups/240 ml red wine

½ cup/175 g tomato paste/purée

1 x 15-oz./400-g can chopped tomatoes

2 x 15-oz./400-g cans black beans

2 oz./55 g good quality bittersweet/dark chocolate, finely chopped

sea salt and cracked black pepper

TO SERVE

crème fraîche

fresh cilantro/coriander leaves

6 limes, quartered

a Dutch oven/large lidded casserole

SERVES 6

LAMB

I have been lucky to have eaten lamb in several different countries, but my real love for lamb came hand in hand with summers spent in the Greek Islands. There, we enjoyed long evening dinners at the beach taverna, eating charcoal grilled lamb that had been slathered in local olive oil, garlic, and rosemary. It was served with a plate of mezze that looked like an artist's palette and a stack of warm grilled pita breads, with a mountain of juicy lemons to squeeze. I never got tired of it.

On the west coast of Ireland in a small town called Roundstone, where the weather is not so balmy, Sean the local butcher would take a delivery of lambs fresh from the hills. They had been feasting on wild thyme and herbs so their meat was sweet and delicious. It needed only the lightest herb salted rub and to be cooked slowly until the meat fell off the bone. Perfect for Sunday lunch.

In Australia, at a good old weekend barbie in the country, large pieces of local lamb had been marinated overnight in wonderful herbed concoctions and were grilled to perfection. Served up with some good red wine, it was another unique taste and experience.

Lamb really is in a league of it's own. Learn to cook with lesser known cuts that are also cheaper. Organic, free-range, and sustainable can be more expensive but the taste is priceless. Your butcher will be only too happy to advise you and give you tips on how to cook them.

The shoulder is really a good place to start and it's less expensive than, say, the leg. It takes on marinades very well, allowing oils and herbs to reach deep into the meat and tenderizing it. I like to use the shoulder cut when I make kebabs. The meat holds up well on the grill/barbecue to high heat and chars beautifully. The fatty bits crisp up and brown, making them the most sought after pieces. It is also a really good cut for stews as, being a heartier piece of meat, it embraces the long, slow cooking in the oven. The meat stays in one piece but is fork tender.

The leg is wonderful roasted in a salt crust rub. It brings out all the flavors and as it slowly cooks the herbs release their aromatics and oils, which mix with the juices of the meat. This cut of the lamb is great for roasting bone in or bone out. If you are roasting it deboned, always rub the inside as well as the outside with a good seasoned rub or paste. This allows the meat to flavor from the inside out. You can then stuff it, roll it up, and tie it ready for the pot.

Lamb, above all other meats, really carries a variety of different seasonings well and lends itself to being cooked in many different ways. Indian seasonings are always good, whether you are making fiery Madras or a more mild-mannered, perfumed Kofta or using a fragrant Indian spice mix.

A rack of lamb is a little more expensive, but they are absolutely delicious and when rubbed with Mediterranean herbs or a spicy fiery Harrissa you will never be disappointed. Grill them to perfection— crispy on the outside and pink and delicate inside. These make the perfect finger food as you can hold them by their wonderful long bones.

In this chapter the marinades, rubs, salts, brines, and seasonings are big and bold and that's what makes cooking with lamb so great.

Lavender SEA SALT RUB

4 generous tablespoons culinary lavender

2 tablespoons good quality coarse sea salt

1 teaspoon ground black pepper

YIELDS ⅓ CUP/
6½ TABLESPOONS

Salt rubs are a fantastic way to get flavor into food. Lavender flowers are so perfumed with rich oil that they release an earthy flavor as they are being cooked. There are several varieties of lavender and all are good to cook with. This lavender salt can also be sprinkled over foods as a finishing salt.

Put all the ingredients in a bowl and mix together.

Store the rub in a glass jar with a tight-fitting lid for up to 6 months.

To use, put the lamb in a ceramic dish, sprinkle over the rub, and rub it into the meat. Cook according to the recipe on page 58, or as preferred. This rub can also be used on chicken or sprinkled as a finishing salt.

Mint and LEMON THYME RUB

½ preserved lemon, finely chopped

1 tablespoon dried mint

2 tablespoons fresh lemon thyme leaves

1 tablespoon fresh rosemary leaves

¼ cup/60 ml extra virgin olive oil

freshly squeezed juice and grated zest of 1 lemon

sea salt and cracked black pepper

YIELDS ⅓ CUP/
6 TABLESPOONS

Drenched in flavors of the Mediterranean, this rub brings out the best in so many foods. So simple and delightful, I use it mostly for lamb, but it is just as good on fish. Dried mint gives a stronger flavor than using fresh and stands up well among these wonderful strong herbs.

Put all the ingredients in a bowl and mix together. Season to taste with salt and pepper and use immediately.

To use, put the lamb in a ceramic dish, sprinkle over the rub, and rub it into the meat. Leave to marinate for 8–24 hours in the fridge. Let the meat come to room temperature, then cook according to the recipe on page 61, or as preferred. This rub can also be used on fish and poultry.

Quick PICKLED CUKES

1 lb./450 g pickling cucumbers

1 tablespoon Kosher/table salt

2 teaspoons brown sugar

½ teaspoon black peppercorns

½ teaspoon pink peppercorns

1 teaspoon yellow mustard seeds

4 fresh bay leaves

1½ cups/350 ml apple cider vinegar

1 sterilized quart/litre glass jar with lid (see page 4)

YIELDS 1 QUART/LITRE

These crunchy cucumber spears are a snap to make and you can keep them in the fridge for 2 weeks. This is a good basic brining recipe for pickling and you can add other spices depending on what vegetable you are using.

Cut the cucumbers into spears and pack them into the glass jar.

In a nonreactive pan, add the salt, sugar, peppercorns, mustard seeds, bay leaves, cider vinegar, and ¼ cup/60 ml water. Bring to a boil over a medium–high heat, then reduce the heat to medium and simmer until the salt and sugar have dissolved.

Pour the hot pickling juice over the cucumbers and fill to the top. Screw the lid on and allow to cool completely before placing in the refrigerator. These will keep for up to 2 weeks.

Lavender SALT CRUSTED
LEG OF LAMB

The beautiful, dainty, bright purple lavender flowers not only look gorgeous but smell gorgeous too. They release wonderful oils, which are filled with flavor. For some reason, lavender and lamb just go together with no explanation needed. Stud the lamb with garlic and rosemary and then coat with the heady lavender salt crust and enjoy.

Preheat the oven to 425°F (220°C) Gas 7.

Rinse the lamb under cold running water and pat dry with a paper towel. Put the leg in a roasting pan and with a sharp knife make shallow incisions over the lamb. Stud with the garlic and rosemary. Rub the lavender sea salt mixture all over the lamb and drizzle with the olive oil.

Roast the lamb in the preheated oven for 15 minutes, then turn down the temperature to 350°F (180°C) Gas 4 and roast for a further 45 minutes. The lamb will be pink in the middle. If you prefer your lamb medium to well done, cook for a further 15 minutes.

Remove the lamb from the oven, cover loosely with kitchen foil, and let rest for 15 minutes before carving.

a 4-lb./1.8-kg leg of lamb, bone in

6 garlic cloves, sliced

leaves from 2 fresh rosemary sprigs

1 recipe of Lavender Sea Salt Rub
(see page 56)

olive oil, to drizzle

SERVES 6

Mint and LEMON THYME
LAMB KEBABS
with QUICK PICKLED CUKES

Chargrilled meats and crunchy pickles are always a good combo. I like to use lamb shoulder as it holds up well on a hot grill and marinating overnight helps tenderize the meat. You could also use leg of lamb. If you have a lemon tree or rosemary bush in your garden, break off branches as these make excellent skewers.

Rinse the lamb under cold running water and pat dry with a paper towel. Cut the lamb into 1¼-inch/3-cm cubes and put in a mixing bowl. Sprinkle the Mint and Lemon Thyme Rub over the lamb and toss to coat evenly. Season with cracked black pepper. (The salt from the preserved lemon should be enough to season.) Cover and refrigerate for 8–24 hours.

Slice the lemon in half, then cut each half into half moons.

Remove the lamb from the fridge and, while still cold, thread onto the prepared skewers or rosemary branches, along with the bay leaves and lemon slices. Cover the skewers and allow to come to room temperature.

On a medium–high grill/barbecue, cook the lamb skewers for 5 minutes, then reduce the heat to medium and turn them over. Cook for a further 6–8 minutes, turning frequently to make sure all the sides are brown and crispy. If you prefer your meat well done, continue to cook the skewers to your preference.

Serve with Quick Pickled Cukes.

1½ lb./680 g lamb shoulder

1 recipe of Mint and Lemon Thyme Rub (see page 56)

1 lemon

6 fresh bay leaves

cracked black pepper

1 recipe of Quick Pickled Cukes (see page 57)

6 x 12-inch/30-cm wooden skewers, soaked in cold water before use, or rosemary branches

YIELDS 6 SKEWERS

Harissa PASTE

2 dried black pasilla chiles
or chile negro

1 dried ancho chile

2 red bell peppers

2 fresh red Serrano chiles

2 teaspoons caraway seeds

2 teaspoons ground cumin

2 tablespoons tomato paste/purée

1 teaspoon smoked paprika

1 garlic clove, roughly chopped

2 tablespoons extra virgin olive oil,
plus a little to seal

sea salt and cracked black pepper

a sterilized glass jar (see page 4)

YIELDS 2 CUPS/480 ML

Harissa is a main staple in my pantry. Although you can easily buy it, it is so easy to make and half the price. I keep it in the fridge in a jar, but I also like to freeze it in an ice cube tray and just grab a cube to flavor stews.

Put the dried chiles in 2 separate bowls and cover with boiling water. Allow to rehydrate for at least 2 hours, or up to 24 hours.

Over a high gas flame, blister the red bell peppers until the skins are black. Set aside and allow to cool, then peel off the skins and roughly chop.

Drain the rehydrated peppers, cut off the stems, and roughly chop.

Put the rehydrated chiles, bell peppers, Serrano chiles, caraway seeds, cumin, tomato paste/purée, paprika, and garlic in a food processor and blend to a rough paste. Stir in the olive oil with a wooden spoon and season with salt and pepper.

Pour the harissa into a sterilized glass jar and pour a little more olive oil on top to seal. Keep in the fridge for up to 1 month.

Use to season stews and pasta, rub on meats before cooking, or even on grilled cheese sandwiches!

Ras-El-Hanout SPICE MIX

1 teaspoon black peppercorns

1 tablespoon green cardamom pods, bashed

1/2 teaspoon whole cloves

1 cinnamon stick, broken up

1 tablespoon cumin seeds

1 1/2 teaspoons dried chili flakes

1/2 teaspoon paprika

1 teaspoon ground allspice

1 teaspoon ground ginger

1/2 teaspoon ground nutmeg

1/2 teaspoon dried garlic powder

1 teaspoon dried rose petals (optional)

YIELDS 1/2 CUP/120 ML

If you ever go to the souks of Marrakech, your senses will be overwhelmed with the smell of spices. The air is filled with them and the traders are spilling over with a kaleidoscope of colorful displays. Ras-El-Hanout means "Head of the Shop" and each trader can mix up to over a 100 spices to make their own recipe. This one is a simpler version but still packs a floral punch.

Roast the peppercorns, cardamom pods, cloves, cinnamon stick, cumin seeds, and chili flakes in a dry cast iron pan set over a medium–high heat for a few minutes, shaking the pan so the spices won't burn. Allow to cool.

Put the roasted spices in an electric spice grinder and process until smooth. Pour into a bowl and add the paprika, allspice, ginger, nutmeg, garlic, and rose petals, if using. Stir well.

Store the spice mix in a glass jar with a tight-fitting lid for up to 6 months.

Use as a seasoning in tagines and stews or as a rub for grilled meats before cooking.

Piri PIRI

6 hot red chiles, roughly chopped

2 teaspoons smoked paprika

4 garlic cloves, roughly chopped

freshly squeezed juice and grated zest of 1 lemon

1/2 cup/120 ml olive oil

sea salt and ground black pepper

YIELDS 1/2 CUP/130 ML

I first started cooking with Piri Piri when I lived in South Africa because of my love of hot peppers and couldn't stop. It's the perfect spicy condiment to enhance marinades, pastes, and brines. Or even just drizzle a little on top of grilled veggies.

Put the chiles, paprika, garlic, lemon zest and juice, and olive oil in a food processor and process until smooth, then season with salt and pepper.

Store the piri piri in a glass jar in the fridge for up to 1 month.

Use piri piri as a wet rub to marinade meats before cooking, or as a condiment with meat, fish, poultry and vegetables.

Harissa and POMEGRANATE
RACK OF LAMB

I always like to flavor lamb with North African spices because they are exotic and packed with flavor. Here, the spices of the harissa run wild with a hint of sweetness from the pomegranate molasses. I cut the lamb rack into double chops, grill them, and serve with a big bowl of herbed couscous.

Rinse the lamb under cold water and pat dry with a paper towel. Cut the racks into double chops and place in a ceramic baking dish.

In a small bowl, mix together the Harissa Paste and pomegranate molasses and pour over the lamb. Rub into the meat, making sure it is well coated. Cover and refrigerate for 8–24 hours.

Remove the lamb from the fridge and stir to make sure all the sauce is on the meat. Allow the meat to come to room temperature.

Preheat a grill/barbecue to medium–high. Put the lamb, skin-side down, on the grill/barbecue and cook for 5 minutes, then flip over. Reduce the heat to medium and cook for another 6–8 minutes. Cook for longer if you prefer your lamb well done.

Plate the chops and sprinkle with the fresh pomegranate seeds.

2 whole racks of lamb

4 tablespoons Harissa Paste
(see page 62)

1 tablespoon pomegranate molasses

seeds from 1 fresh pomegranate

SERVES 6

Date and OLIVE
LAMB TAGINE

This hearty stew is laced with rich Moroccan spices that will fill the air with perfume when cooking. I like to serve this straight from the oven in the pot it's cooked in, with a pile of grilled flatbreads. Be generous with your mint leaves—they give a cool note to the spices.

Put the lamb pieces in a ceramic bowl and sprinkle with the Ras-El-Hanout. Mix thoroughly, making sure you coat all the meat with the spices. Cover and refrigerate for 8–24 hours.

Remove the lamb from the fridge and bring to room temperature. Preheat the oven to 350°F (180°C) Gas 4.

Put an oven-proof dish with a tight-fitting lid over a medium–high heat. Heat the olive oil in the pan and sauté the shallots and garlic until golden brown. Add the meat and sear on all sides, then add the bay leaves and saffron and mix together. Pour in the tomatoes and Harissa Paste and stir to combine.

Bring the tagine to a boil then turn off the heat. Put the lid on the pot and place it in the preheated oven. Cook for 45 minutes, then add the dates and olives and continue to cook for a further 45 minutes.

Remove the tagine from the oven and serve in a bowl, sprinkled with the torn mint leaves.

1½ lb./680 g lamb shoulder, cut into 1¼-inch/3-cm pieces

2 tablespoons Ras-El-Hanout Spice Mix (see page 63)

2 tablespoons olive oil

2 shallots, finely sliced

2 garlic cloves, finely chopped

2 dried bay leaves

½ teaspoon ground saffron threads

1 x 28-oz. can/2 x 400-g cans chopped tomatoes

½ teaspoon Harissa Paste (see page 63)

¾ cup/100 g pitted dates

¾ cup/75 g green olives

a large bunch of fresh mint, stalks removed and leaves torn

SERVES 4—6

Indian SPICED RUB

1 teaspoon ground cumin

1 cinnamon stick, broken into pieces

2 tablespoons cardamom pods, bashed

1 teaspoon whole cloves

1 teaspoon ground turmeric

1 teaspoon smoked paprika

1 teaspoon garam masala

YIELDS ¼ CUP/4 TABLESPOONS

This spicy rub goes with everything, and adding oil or yogurt turns it into a paste that can be spread under the skin of chicken or on fish. I love to mix up the spices in this basic recipe and change it to Madras or Tandoori.

Heat a cast iron pan over a medium–high heat and add all the ingredients. Roast for 3–4 minutes, stirring constantly so they don't burn. Transfer the roasted spices to an electric spice grinder and process to a coarse powder.

Store the rub in a glass jar with a tight-fitting lid for up to 6 months.

To use, put the meat in a ceramic dish, sprinkle over the spice rub, and rub it into the meat. Leave to marinate for 8–24 hours in the fridge. Let the meat come to room temperature, then cook according to the recipe on page 70, or as preferred. This spice rub can also be used on beef, fish, and poultry.

Full-bodied MERLOT MARINADE

1 x 75-cl bottle Merlot

2 tablespoons tomato paste/purée

4 garlic cloves, roughly chopped

1 tablespoon herbes de Provence

2 dried bay leaves

2 tablespoons olive oil

sea salt and cracked black pepper

YIELDS 3¼ CUPS/800 ML

If you love red wine, this marinade is for you. Use a full-bodied bottle of Merlot as you want the meat to have that wonderful flavor seeping through it. A bonus with this recipe is that, when you are ready to cook the meat, you can reduce the excess marinade by half over a high heat and you have a wonderful lively jus.

Put the Merlot, tomato paste/purée, garlic, herbes de Provence, bay leaves, and olive oil in a blender or food processor and process until well mixed. Season with salt and pepper.

Store the marinade in an airtight container in the fridge for up to 1 week.

To use, put the meat in a ceramic dish, pour over the marinade, and leave to marinate for 8–24 hours in the fridge. Let the meat come to room temperature, then cook as preferred.

Greek LEMON YOGURT MARINADE

1 cup/240 ml Greek yogurt

freshly squeezed juice and grated zest of 1 lemon

2 garlic cloves, finely chopped

2 tablespoons oregano leaves

1 teaspoon dried mint leaves

2 tablespoons olive oil

sea salt and cracked black pepper

YIELDS 1¼ CUPS/300 ML

Greek yogurt is thicker than regular and is ideal for using in marinades because of this. It doesn't tend to run off when you are cooking and gives a nice coating. I like to use a variety of herbs and spices depending on what I am cooking—simply adding curry powder to a tub of yogurt is a delicious way to marinate chicken.

Whisk all the ingredients together in a ceramic or glass bowl.

Cover and refrigerate until ready to use.

Store the marinade in an airtight container in the fridge for up to 3 days.

To use, put the meat in a ceramic dish, pour over the marinade, and leave to marinate for 8–24 hours in the fridge. Let the meat come to room temperature, then cook as preferred. This marinade can also be used on chicken.

Indian SPICED
LAMB LEG STEAKS
with TANDOORI BREADS *and* RAITA

2 leg of lamb bone-in steaks (about 2 lb./900 g), cut 1½ inches/4 cm thick

sea salt and cracked black pepper

3 tablespoons Indian Spice Rub (see page 68)

olive oil, to drizzle

RAITA

1 cup/240 ml Greek yogurt

1 cup/120 g grated cucumber

1 garlic cloves, finely chopped

a small bunch of fresh mint, stalks removed and leaves torn

sea salt

TO SERVE

Tandoori Indian breads, such as naan

fresh cilantro/coriander, to garnish

lime wedges

SERVES 4

Sometimes the whole leg of lamb is too much, so I ask my butcher to cut thick steaks from the leg and then I marinate them overnight. This way, all these wonderful Indian spices are flavoring the meat. They are great thrown on an outside grill and then sliced up and tossed onto Indian breads.

Rinse the lamb under cold water and pat dry with a paper towel. Lay the steaks in a ceramic dish and season with salt and pepper. Sprinkle the Indian Spice Rub over the meat and rub it in, making sure all the meat is coated. Drizzle with a little olive oil, then cover and refrigerate for 8–24 hours.

To make the Raita, put all the ingredients in a mixing bowl and mix thoroughly. Cover and refrigerate until ready to serve.

Remove the lamb from the fridge and bring to room temperature.

Heat the grill to medium–high. Lay the lamb steaks on the grill and cook for 4-5 minutes each side for medium rare. Cook longer if you prefer your lamb well done. Remove the steaks to a wooden board, cover, and rest for 10 minutes.

While the lamb steaks are resting, grill the tandoori breads until crispy and golden brown. Arrange on a platter.

Slice the lamb into thin strips and pile on top of the breads. Drizzle over the juices and top with spoonfuls of raita. Sprinkle with fresh cilantro/coriander leaves and serve with lime wedges.

POULTRY

Poultry are excellent for all seasonings and any type of cooking. They roast, poach, grill, and stir fry perfectly. They enjoy being marinated, rubbed, pasted, and buttered. When buying poultry, make sure it does come from a reliable source. Again local, organic, sustainable are key. Most farmers' markets have a purveyor who is selling chickens and ducks as well as fresh eggs.

I always like to buy whole birds and either cut them up for different dishes or cook as they are. The main benefit of buying whole is that you get a bonus by making stock with the carcass. You can then either freeze it for a later use, or make soup or a wonderful risotto. A lot of meals can come out of one bird, which is a very economical way to shop.

Turkeys and chickens really benefit from overnight brining. It tenderizes and flavors the meat. Turkeys have such large cavities that they tend to dry out when cooking. I like to rub robust butters between the skin and the breast. I then sprinkle a salt rub over the skin as this ensures crispiness on the outside and tender juicy meat on the inside.

The wings and drummetes are really great to marinade in a jerk paste then throw on the grill. As they cook over the hot coals, the skins caramelize and crisp up, making for a tasty morsel while waiting for the main event. Don't forget to squeeze lashings of fresh lime juice over them just before digging in.

A really good way to grill/barbecue a whole chicken is to butterfly it and open it like a book. You cut along either side of the backbone with a pair of kitchen scissors then remove the bone and flatten the chicken. Marinate it or season with a herbed rub or paste, then cook on the grill. It will cut your cooking time by half.

Ducks are really good for making skewers as the breast meat is thick and covered in a layer of fat which melts when cooked, protecting the delicate meat inside. As they cook, brush the skewers with a glaze or marinade, ensuring a further delicious layer of flavor. A whole duck also has a large cavity and tends to really dry out when roasting, so use the same technique as with a turkey, rubbing flavored butter under the skin. I like to pair the duck with sweet but tart earthy flavors, such as cherries and pomegranates, and make them into a marinade and glaze. They work well with the flavor of the duck. Any kind of Asian mix of ginger, soy, tamarind, and allspice works excellently with this meat, so get in the kitchen and have fun mixing the flavors up.

My favorite way of seasoning poultry is with pastes as they are so simple. I like to open the fridge and see what can be used. This is where you can get really creative and I find there are never any mistakes. Grilling the meat really helps caramelize the pastes, especially if honey or maple syrup is involved.

Don't they say great things come in small packages and I would say this is absolutely true about quail. This is a little bird with a mighty big taste. I tend to use Moroccan or Asian pastes and rubs and either grill or roast in the oven until they are dark golden brown and crispy. They are exquisite served over a bed of jeweled couscous or piping hot jasmine rice, with the juices poured liberally over them.

Jamaican JERK PASTE

8 Habanero or Scotch Bonnet chiles

a 4-inch/10-cm piece of fresh ginger, peeled and roughly chopped

1 yellow onion, roughly chopped

8 garlic cloves, peeled and smashed

4 sprigs fresh thyme, roughly chopped

1 tablespoon ground cinnamon

1 tablespoon ground allspice

1 tablespoon grated nutmeg

3 tablespoons molasses

¼ cup/60 ml Jamaican rum

sea salt and ground black pepper

YIELDS 2 CUPS/480 ML

This recipe hails from Jamaica and Habanero chiles are the key ingredient. They are a beautiful bright orange color and look like tiny lanterns. Supposedly the hottest chiles in the world, you may want to use gloves when handling them. The sweetness of the other spices makes for an incredible explosion of flavors. You can use this paste on anything and it is perfect for any barbecue dish.

Put all the ingredients in a food processor or blender and process to a coarse purée.

Store the paste in an airtight container in the fridge for up to 2 weeks.

To use, put the meat in a ceramic dish, pour over the paste, and rub it into the meat. Leave to marinate for 8–24 hours in the fridge. Let the meat come to room temperature, then cook according to the recipe on page 78, or as preferred.

Adobo MARINADE

4 garlic cloves, peeled and smashed

1 teaspoon Harrissa Paste (see page 62)

2 teaspoons dried oregano

2 teaspoons dried thyme

½ teaspoon ground cinnamon

¼ cup/60 ml red wine vinegar

¼ cup/60 ml olive oil

½ teaspoon sea salt

½ teaspoon ground black pepper

YIELDS SCANT ¾ CUP/200 ML

A friend of mine inspired me to come up with this recipe. She made Chicken Adobo for dinner one night and, along with the great company, it was one of my favorite eating experiences. Let the poultry or meat marinade for as long as you can, preferably overnight.

Put all the ingredients in a food processor and process until smooth.

Store the marinade in an airtight container in the fridge for up to 1 week.

To use, put the poultry in a ceramic dish, pour over the marinade, and leave to marinate for 8–24 hours in the fridge. Let the meat come to room temperature, then cook as preferred.

Cherry and POMEGRANATE GLAZE

2 cups/450 g dark cherries (such as Bing cherries), pitted

2 tablespoons pomegranate molasses

2 teaspoons dried thyme

2 teaspoons dried rosemary

sea salt and cracked black pepper

YIELDS ABOUT 2 CUPS/480 ML

Cherries are a great fruit to make a glaze with—they are sweet, but not too sweet, and they hold up well for cooking. Adding the pomegranate molasses and the dried herbs makes for a syrupy sweet and savory glaze, which is a perfect partner for duck and gamey poultry.

Put the cherries and pomegranate molasses in a food processor and pulse until you have a chunky sauce. Pour the sauce into a ceramic bowl and stir in the thyme and rosemary. Season with salt and pepper.

Store the glaze in an airtight container in the fridge for up to 2 weeks.

Use according to the recipe on page 81, or marinate poultry or meat in the glaze overnight, then remove from the glaze and cook, as preferred. Simmer the remaining glaze for 10 minutes to reduce, then serve on the side of the poultry or meat. This glaze also works well with lamb.

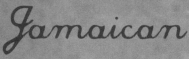
Jamaican

JERK CHICKEN

4½ lb./2 kg chicken wings

1 recipe of Jamaican Jerk Paste
(see page 76)

fresh limes, to squeeze

SERVES 6

This is a perfect BBQ accompaniment. Have a big plate of jerk chicken wings for everyone to eat while they are waiting for the long-cooked meats on the grill. Hot Caribbean flavors doused with freshly squeezed limes make you feel that you are on the beach. Serve with icy cold beers.

Wash the chicken wings under cold water and pat dry with a paper towel. Put the wings in a large glass or ceramic bowl and pierce all over with a sharp knife. (You want the marinade to get deep inside the chicken.) Pour over the Jamaican Jerk Paste and rub into the wings with your hands, being careful not to touch your face. Cover the baking dish with plastic wrap/clingfilm and refrigerate for 24 hours. This is a long marinade and mustn't be hurried.

After this time, remove the chicken wings from the fridge and take off the plastic wrap/clingfilm. Toss one more time to make sure they are all well covered with the jerk seasoning.

Put the wings on a medium–hot grill/barbecue and cook for 6–8 minutes. Turn the grill/barbecue down and continue to cook the wings for a further 8 minutes, turning frequently until they are cooked through and crispy on the outside.

Serve the chicken wings on a large platter and squeeze over the fresh limes. Eat immediately.

Cherry POMEGRANATE
GRILLED DUCK SKEWERS

When cherry season comes along, I can't eat enough of them. Although I love all cherries, dark ruby red Bing cherries are my favorite. Here, I marinate duck breasts overnight in a fruity herbed mixture, then grill them until crispy. These bite-size skewers are perfect to serve with drinks at weekend barbecues.

Wash the duck breasts in cold water and pat dry with a paper towel. Put the duck on a board and slice crosswise into 1½-inch/4-cm strips.

Pour the Cherry and Pomegranate Glaze into a large glass bowl and add the duck strips. Stir well to make sure the duck is completely covered in the marinade, then cover and refrigerate overnight.

Remove the duck from the fridge. While the strips are still cold, thread them onto the prepared wooden skewers, cover, and set aside until they come up to room temperature.

Pour the remaining marinade into a small saucepan and bring to a boil. Reduce the heat and simmer the sauce for 10 minutes.

Lay the duck skewers, fat side down, on a medium–high grill/barbecue. Cook for 5 minutes then turn the skewers over. Reduce the heat to medium and cook for a further 5 minutes, until crispy on the outside and cooked through.

Pour the warm marinade into a small bowl and serve with the skewers.

2 duck breasts (about 1 lb./450 g)

1 recipe of Cherry & Pomegranate Glaze (see page 77)

16 x 8-inch/20-cm wooden skewers, soaked in cold water before use

YIELDS 16 SKEWERS

Italian HERBED RUB

1 tablespoon fresh rosemary leaves

2 tablespoons lemon thyme leaves

a small bunch of fresh flat-leaf parsley, finely chopped

freshly squeezed juice and grated zest of 1 Meyer lemon

¼ cup/60 ml olive oil

sea salt and cracked black pepper

YIELDS SCANT ¾ CUP/180 ML

Rubs are a great way to season food. By adding a little oil, you can make a dry rub into a paste. If seasoning poultry, rub the spices under the skin as well as on top.

Put all the ingredients in a bowl and mix together. Season with salt and pepper.

Store the rub in an airtight container in the fridge for up to to 3 days.

To use, put the poultry in a ceramic dish, sprinkle over the rub, and rub it into the meat. Leave to marinate for 8–24 hours in the fridge. Let the poultry come to room temperature, then cook according to the recipe on page 84, or as preferred. This rub can also be used on beef and fish.

Mediterranean BRINE

½ cup/65 g Kosher/table salt

1 large sprig fresh rosemary

2 garlic cloves

¼ cup/60 ml white balsamic vinegar

1 tablespoon black peppercorns

YIELDS 2¼ QUARTS/LITRES

This is not a complicated brine—the flavors are simple so as to enrich the final dish but not to take over. The rosemary and balsamic give the brine a Mediterranean touch, which is perfect for all poultry.

Put all the ingredients in a large pan with 2 quarts/litres water and set over a medium–high heat. Bring to a boil and stir until all the salt has dissolved. Remove from the heat and let cool completely before using.

To use, put the poultry in a large pan and pour over the brine, making sure the meat is submerged (add more cold water if needed). Cover and put in the fridge overnight, then rinse the meat and cook according to the recipe on page 84, or as preferred. This brine can also be used for beef and lamb.

Escabeche MARINADE

½ cup/120 ml extra virgin oil

1 yellow onion, halved and thinly sliced

4 garlic cloves, finely chopped

4 bay leaves

a pinch of saffron

6 sprigs fresh marjoram

6 sprigs fresh thyme

1 cup/240 ml medium-dry sherry

¼ cup/60 ml white wine vinegar

coarse sea salt and cracked black pepper

YIELDS 2 CUPS/480 ML

Escabeche is the Spanish method of pickling or marinating cooked food in vinegar, wine, or a citrus sauce. It is perfect in the summer as you can make it, refrigerate it, and go to the beach and when you come home serve it straight from the fridge with a tossed salad. It's in the poultry chapter but you can use it for seafood and vegetables, too.

Put ¼ cup/60 ml of the olive oil, the onion, and garlic in a sauté pan set over a medium–high heat. Cook for about 5 minutes, until the onions are soft and have taken on a golden brown color.

Add the bay leaves, saffron, marjoram, and thyme to the pan and continue to cook for a further 2–3 minutes. Pour in the remaining olive oil and the sherry and vinegar and simmer for 10 minutes. Season with salt and pepper and remove from the heat.

Pour the marinade over your prepared cooked chicken. Cover and refrigerate until ready to eat. Serve cold or at room temperature.

Italian ROASTED
CORNISH GAME HENS
with PROSCIUTTO

2 Cornish game hens/poussin

1 recipe of Mediterranean Brine
(see page 83)

1 large shallot, halved

1 recipe of Italian Herbed Rub
(see page 82)

4–6 slices prosciutto

kitchen twine

SERVES 4

If ever there was a dish perfect for a lazy Sunday lunch it's these wonderfully seasoned hens. Brined overnight, rubbed all over with fresh herbs, topped with salty prosciutto, then roasted: it couldn't be better. I serve them with a crisp green salad and then relax and dream of Italy.

Rinse the hens under cold running water. Put them in a large saucepan and pour over the Mediterranean Brine, making sure they are submerged (add more cold water if needed). Place a plate or small pan lid on top of the hens to keep them submerged, then cover and refrigerate overnight.

Preheat the oven to 375°F (190°C) Gas 5.

Remove the hens from the fridge, rinse under cold water, and pat dry with a paper towel. Put them in a roasting pan and stuff with the shallot halves. Pour over the Italian Herbed Rub, making sure to get it into the cavities. Push it under the breast skin and rub all over. Lay the prosciutto slices over the hens and truss the legs with kitchen twine.

Roast the hens in the preheated oven for 15 minutes, then turn down the heat to 350°F (180°C) Gas 4. Cook for a further 45 minutes, basting half way through, until the juices run clear.

Remove the hens from the oven and cover loosely with kitchen foil. Let rest for 15 minutes before serving.

Thai LEMONGRASS PASTE

a 2-inch/5-cm piece of galangal, peeled and roughly chopped

2 stalks fresh lemongrass, bashed and roughly chopped

6 Kaffir lime leaves

4 birds' eye chiles, roughly chopped

2 tablespoons honey

2 tablespoons fish sauce

1 teaspoon Sriracha sauce or hot sauce

freshly squeezed juice and grated zest of 2 limes

3 tablespoons vegetable oil

a large bunch of fresh cilantro/coriander, chopped

YIELDS 1 CUP/250 ML

This is a wonderful, fresh-tasting paste that works really well with poultry. The vibrant aromas of lemongrass, lime leaves, and lemon fill the air. I am using galangal, which is part of the ginger family and has a strong punch to it. If you can't easily find it, simply substitute fresh ginger.

Put all the ingredients in a blender or food processor and process to a thick paste.

Store the paste in an airtight container in the fridge for up to 1 week.

Use to season curries or rub on poultry before cooking. This paste can also be used on beef, pork, or fish.

Spicy Ginger and ANISE MARINADE

2 cups/240 ml soy sauce

1 tablespoon fresh ginger, peeled and finely chopped or grated

3 star anise

2 tablespoons toasted sesame oil

1 teaspoon dry mustard

1 teaspoon dried chili flakes

2 teaspoons Chinese five spice

¼ cup/60 ml orange blossom honey

1 scallion/spring onion, finely chopped

YIELDS 2½ CUPS/600 ML

I like to keep the Asian flavors as simple as possible, making sure to get the balance of salty, sweet, and spicy just right. I use dried chiles in the recipe but you can use fresh chiles too. This is a perfect match for chicken and pork and takes a second to throw together.

Put all the ingredients in a glass bowl and whisk together.

Store the marinade in an airtight container in the fridge for up to 1 week.

To use, put the meat in a ceramic dish, pour over the marinade, and leave to marinate for 8–24 hours in the fridge. Let the meat come to room temperature, then cook according to the recipe on page 89, or as preferred. This marinade can also be used on pork.

Tamarind, Chipotle, and
GINGER MARINADE

¼ cup/4 tablespoons tamarind paste

¼ cup/60 ml honey

¼ cup/60 ml olive oil

4 garlic cloves, finely chopped

2 tablespoons grated fresh ginger

2 teaspoons chipotle chili powder

½ teaspoon coarse sea salt

¼ teaspoon ground black pepper

YIELDS 1 CUP/250 ML

Tamarind has a wonderful sourness which, matched with chiles and ginger, livens up any marinade. It's a great thirst quencher and is used widely in warmer climates for flavoring drinks. This is great for grilling chicken, as the marinade caramelizes when cooked over a hot grill.

Put all the ingredients in a bowl and mix together.

Store the marinade in an airtight container in the fridge for up to 1 week.

To use, put the meat in a ceramic dish, pour over the marinade, and leave to marinate for 8–24 hours in the fridge. Let the meat come to room temperature, then cook as preferred. This marinade can also be used on beef and fish.

Clay POT
SLOW ROASTED CHICKEN

Using a Chinese clay pot is a fun way to cook chicken, but if you don't have one, any ovenproof pot with a tight fitting lid will work—just make sure the pot is a similar size to the chicken. Bursting with flavor, it's always a treat. I like to serve this over jasmine rice or noodles that will soak up all the delicious juices. The leftovers make a mouthwatering stock for chicken dumpling soup.

Wash the chicken under cold water and pat dry with a paper towel. Fill the cavity with the ginger, garlic, and cinnamon stick. Using kitchen twine, tie the legs together tightly, then place the chicken into the clay pot, breast-side down. Pour the marinade over the chicken, put the lid on the pot, and put in the refrigerator for 8–24 hours to allow the marinade flavors to soak in.

After this time, remove the clay pot from the fridge and turn the chicken over so the breast is now facing up. Cover and let the chicken come up to room temperature.

Preheat the oven to 300°F (150°C) Gas 2.

Put the covered pot in the preheated oven and slowly cook for 2 hours. When done, remove from the oven and let rest for 15 minutes.

Take the chicken out of the pot and place on a wooden board. Carve the tender meat. Serve the chicken, spooning over the remaining juices.

a 3½-lb./1.5-kg chicken

a 3-inch/7.5-cm piece of fresh ginger, peeled and cut into 4 knobs

4 garlic cloves, bashed

1 cinnamon stick

1 recipe of Spicy Ginger and Anise Marinade (see page 86)

kitchen twine

a large clay pot

SERVES 4

Thai LEMONGRASS
QUAIL

Thai herbs and spices are delicious with delicate quail.
I grill them or roast them in the oven. Either way, they
are crispy brown and bursting with flavor. I serve each
guest a bowl of jasmine rice with the quail propped on
top, with juicy lime wedges to squeeze.

Rinse the quail under cold water and pat dry with a paper towel. Put
them in a ceramic baking dish and pour over the Thai Lemongrass Paste.
Rub the paste into the quail on both sides, then cover and refrigerate for
6–8 hours, or overnight.

After this time, remove the quail from the fridge and leave to come up to
room temperature.

Preheat a gas or charcoal grill/barbecue or a grill pan on the stove top
over a medium–high heat.

Lay the quail on the heated grill/barbecue, skin side down, and cook for
8 minutes per side until cooked through. When done, remove from the
grill, cover, and let stand for 10 minutes.

Serve the quail with lime wedges for squeezing over.

8 quail, halved lengthwise along the
backbones

1 recipe of Thai Lemongrass Paste
(see page 86)

6 limes, quartered, to serve

SERVES 4

FISH

Buying seafood can be a little overwhelming unless you have a wonderful local fishmonger who can tell you what is fresh, seasonal, and sustainable. Here are some general tips, which will help you navigate the sea of fish.

Buy fish on the same day that you are eating it, or up to 1 day ahead and store in the refrigerator. When choosing fish, make sure the eyes are bright and the skin firm and shiny. Fish portions that are already gutted should again be firm and moist. Stay away from fish that looks dry with dull skins. Most important of all, fresh fish does not smell so stay away from any kind of unpleasant odor.

When choosing mussels or clams, choose only those that are closed and their shells are intact. Store them in the refrigerator for up to 1 day in a bowl with a damp cloth to cover them.

Shrimp/prawns should have firm shells, and be bright and juicy looking. If you are buying frozen seafood, especially shrimp/prawns, look at the package to see the country of origin. Some countries do not adhere to healthy farming practices and can also harm other marine life and the environment. Stay up to date on what fish are abundant and local. You can do this very easily by checking out the internet and the different sites that offer this information.

There are so many ways to cook fish and getting seasoning into them. Marinating fish is an excellent way of doing this. However, don't leave the fish in the sauce for longer than 30 minutes, otherwise the flesh starts to break up. The exception to this is ceviche, as the brine needs to permeate the fish to cook it in the acidic juices.

Fun ways when grilling smaller fish, such as sardines, are to stuff them and roll them in vine leaves or proscuitto. This way, although they are very small, they stay together on the grill/barbecue and are easy to turn over without them falling apart.

Dry rubs are a quick way to season fish fillets. You can quickly mix together a herb or spice mix with what you have in your pantry. Rub it over the fish, the, pan-fry in olive oil or butter, which adds a nice vibrancy to the dish. By adding oil to the dry mixes, you can quickly turn them into pastes.

Flavored butters are perfect for dolloping over fish toward the end of grilling and roasting. Imagine a beautiful piece of roasted fish straight out of a piping hot oven, with a dab of herbed butter melting and coating it, bringing out even more flavor.

One of the best ways to entertain in the summer is to cook up a New England Clambake. Spill it out onto tables in the back yard covered with newspaper. Accompany it with crusty baguettes and icy cold beers and I can guarantee you everyone will be very impressed, and happy.

Ceviches are great to prepare when the weather is hot. They are so simple to make. When using fresh lime or lemon leaves, crush them in your hands as this releases the wonderful fresh aromatic oils that flavor the marinade. Use the Lime Leaf and Citrus Ceviche Brine recipe in this chapter and change up the seafood to use fresh shrimp/prawns, calamari, or any kind of fish that you like. Just make sure the fish is very fresh (not frozen) and grade A—this is definitely the time to ask your fishmonger for his recommendations.

Homemade OLD BAY SEASONING

4 whole green cardamom pods

4 dried bay leaves

1 teaspoon yellow mustard powder

1 teaspoon yellow mustard seeds

1 teaspoon celery seeds

1 teaspoon cracked black pepper

1 teaspoon sea salt

1 teaspoon paprika

½ teaspoon whole cloves

½ teaspoon dried garlic powder

½ teaspoon ground nutmeg

½ teaspoon ground allspice

½ teaspoon chili powder

YIELDS ¼ CUP/4 TABLEPOONS

I have a great fondness for Old Bay Seasoning, especially the yellow and blue tin: it's a bright star on the spice shelf. Created in the 1940s in Baltimore, Maryland, where there is an abundance of seafood, it's an American classic. Although we will never know exactly what goes into this secret mix, here is a quick version.

Put all the ingredients into an electric spice grinder and process until you have a fine powder.

Store the seasoning in a glass jar with a tight-fitting lid for up to 6 months.

To use, add 1 or 2 tablespoons to clambakes, steamed crab, fish stews and soups, or use to spice up marinades.

Friday night FISH FRY

1 cup/150 g cornmeal/polenta

1 teaspoon celery salt

1 teaspoon dried garlic powder

½ teaspoon Spanish smoked paprika (pimentòn)

½ teaspoon chili powder

½ teaspoon sea salt

½ teaspoon ground white pepper

YIELDS SCANT 1¼ CUPS/300 ML

Friday night is all about the fish fry in the Midwest. A hearty plate of fish and fries with a side of slaw or sauerkraut is served up with an icy cold beer. After all the eating is done, it's off for a spot of polka dancing to work it all off. I have spiced this traditional recipe up and use it for coating chicken too.

Put all the ingredients in a mixing bowl and stir well.

Store in a glass jar with a tight-fitting lid for up to 1 month.

To use, coat fish fillets in the seasoning and fry as usual.

Lime leaf and CITRUS CEVICHE BRINE

6 lime leaves, bruised

freshly squeezed juice and grated zest of 1 pink grapefruit, 1 orange, and 2 limes

½ teaspoon sea salt

YIELDS 2 CUPS/480 ML

This delicate ceviche brine is perfumed with lime leaves. Rub them between your hands to bruise them, which will release the wonderful oils and florals of the leaves. This brine is made especially for a summer's day, when outside eating is a must.

Whisk all the ingredients together in a glass bowl and use according to the recipe on page 100.

New England HOME
CLAMBAKE

Bring the beach to your kitchen by simply layering seafood in a large pan for this home clambake. Cover an outside table with newspaper and pour the contents of the pot out. Dig in armed only with lobster crackers. Fun summer outdoor eating.

Set the stock pot over a medium–high heat. Pour in 1 cup/240 ml water and add the wine, seasoning, salt, and garlic and bring to a boil.

Add the onion and potatoes to the pan, then place the lobsters on top. Cover and cook for 15–20 minutes. Add the the clams and corn and continue to cook for a further 8–10 minutes with the lid tightly on. Check to see if the clam shells have opened, if not continue to cook until they have.

Remove the pan from the heat and carefully strain off the cooking liquid. Tip the remaining contents of the pot onto the prepared table or transfer to a large platter. Serve with the melted butter, crusty bread, and lemons and limes to squeeze over.

2 cups/240 ml white wine

2½ tablespoons of Homemade Old Bay Seasoning (see page 96)

1 teaspoon coarse sea salt

4 garlic cloves, bashed

1 red onion, roughly chopped

2 lb./900 g baby potatoes, halved

2 lobsters, about 1½–2 lb./ 680–900 g each

2 dozen Manila clams

4 fresh corn on the cob, cut into 4 parts

a small bunch of fresh tarragon or flat-leaf parsley, roughly chopped

TO SERVE

2 sticks/225 g butter, melted

crusty bread

3 lemons and 3 limes, cut into wedges

a stock pot or pasta pot with a tight-fitting lid

SERVES 4–6

HALIBUT CEVICHE
with Citrus CEVICHE BRINE

1 lb./450 g sushi-grade fresh halibut

2 shallots, finely chopped

1 recipe of Lime Leaf and Citrus Ceviche Brine (see page 97)

1 pink grapefruit, peeled and sliced thinly

1 orange, peeled and sliced thinly

2 limes, peeled peeled and sliced thinly

fresh fennel pollen (see page 19) and fennel flowers, to sprinkle

½ teaspoon pink Himalayan salt

¼ cup/60 ml extra virgin olive oil

SERVES 4—6

I absolutely adore preparing this ceviche. It is so beautiful and delicate to look at with the jewel-like tones of the fruit. Lime, pink grapefruit, and oranges make it look almost too glamorous to eat. Sprinkle over a few fennel flowers to finish, or any other herbal flowers you have growing in the garden.

Rinse the halibut under cold water and pat dry with a paper towel. Lay the fish on a wooden board and slice wafer thin.

Arrange the fish in a ceramic dish in a single layer. Sprinkle over the shallots and pour over the Lime Leaf and Citrus Ceviche Brine, making sure all the fish is submerged in the liquid. Cover and place in the fridge for 3 hours.

After this time, remove the halibut from the fridge and arrange on a platter. Top with the citrus slices. Sprinkle with fennel pollen and flowers. Season with the salt, drizzle with the olive oil, and serve.

Charmoula PASTE

1 tablespoon ground coriander

1 tablespoon ground cumin

4 garlic cloves, finely chopped

1 preserved lemon, finely chopped

a large bunch of fresh flat-leaf parsley, finely chopped

1 teaspoon dried chili flakes

½ teaspoon smoked paprika

a good pinch saffron threads

2 tablespoons freshly squeezed lime juice

½ cup/120 ml olive oil

YIELDS 1½ CUPS/360 ML

Charmoula is a wonderful mixture of north African inspired spices with a good pinch of saffron. I think this mix was made for fish and it never ceases to disappoint me or my guests. Serve with grilled fish and a big pile of couscous.

Put all the ingredients in a bowl and whisk together.

Can be stored in a glass jar with a tight-fitting lid for up to 1 week.

Use with fish according to the recipe on page 104, or add 1–2 tablespoons to vegetable and fish stews. You could also brush over chicken or lamb and marinate for 8–24 hours in the fridge. Let the meat come to room temperature, then cook as preferred.

Black Olive STUFFING

1 cup/80 g toasted breadcrumbs

½ cup/60 g cured black olives, pitted and chopped

a small bunch of fresh flat-leaf parsley, roughly chopped

a small bunch of fresh oregano leaves

½ cup/120 ml olive oil

sea salt and cracked black pepper

YIELDS 2¾ CUPS/650 ML

This is a simple and fast stuffing, which can be put together in moments. The saltiness of the cured black olives and the aromatics of the herbs give it a wonderful Mediterranean feel. It can be used for all fish and meats. Change it up by using different kinds of olives, such as Kalamata or Niçoise.

Put the breadcrumbs, olives, parsley, and oregano in a bowl. Pour in the olive oil, a little at a time (you may not need it all), and stir until the stuffing begins to bind together. Season with salt and pepper.

Store the stuffing in an airtight container in the fridge for up to 1–2 days.

Use the stuffing according to the recipe on page 107, or to stuff any fish or meats before cooking.

Red CURRY PASTE

2 tablespoons roughly chopped
fresh ginger

6 red fresh chiles, roughly chopped

4 birds' eye chiles, roughly chopped

6 lime leaves, roughly chopped

1 stalk fresh lemongrass,
roughly chopped

4 garlic cloves, peeled and bashed

2 teaspoons Sambal Oelek
(ground fresh chile paste)

2 tablespoons fish sauce

1 teaspoon shrimp paste

freshly squeezed juice and grated
zest of 1 lime

1 teaspoon palm sugar

2 tablespoons vegetable oil

YIELDS SCANT ¾ CUP/180 ML

This may look like hard work with the list of ingredients,
but once you have made this paste you can store it in the
fridge for a week. It's fiery and filled with aromatics, but
once you add it to coconut milk for a curry it becomes
a wonderful creamy sauce.

Put all the ingredients in a food processor or blender and process to a
coarse paste.

Store the paste in an airtight container in the fridge for up to 1 week.

Use to spice up curries, soups, or in a dressing for an Asian salad, or rub
onto fish and allow to marinate before cooking as preferred.

Spiced RED SNAPPER
with CHARMOULA

I love fish cooked over hot coals—it's a summer classic which reminds me of fishing and then cooking the catch on the beach. Snapper is an excellent fish to grill with. It's sturdy and the meat just falls off the bones. Always have lots of freshly cut lemons and limes on hand to squeeze over the fish.

Wash the snapper under cold water and pat dry. Lay the fish on a platter big enough to hold them all.

Stuff the snapper with the sliced lemons and brush the fish inside and out with the Charmoula Paste. Season with salt and pepper.

Preheat the grill/barbecue or set a grill pan over a medium–high heat.

Lay the fish on the hot grill/barbecue and cook for 8–10 minutes on each side, depending on the thickness of the fish, until the flesh is cooked through. Remove the fish from the grill/barbecue or grill pan, cover with foil and let rest for 5 minutes.

Serve the fish with the lemon and lime quarters.

4 red snapper

2 lemons, thinly sliced

1 recipe of Charmoula Paste
(see page 102)

sea salt and cracked black pepper

2 lemons, quartered, to serve

2 limes, quartered, to serve

SERVES 4

Grilled VINE LEAF WRAPPED
SARDINES

This recipe reminds me of many happy hours spent eating in Greece in wonderful little tavernas dotted along the beaches. They were long lazy lunches, eaten with your toes in the sand under canopies protecting you from the midday sun, and sipping icy cold retsina. The the rest of the day was spent swimming and lazing around.

With a sharp knife, cut along the bottom of the sardines where they have been gutted. Rinse under cold water and pat dry with a paper towel.

Lay the vine leaves down on a work surface with the stem facing upward. Place a sardine on each leaf, then stuff each of the sardines with the Black Olive Stuffing. Fold the stem end of the leaf over the fish and tuck in both sides, then roll up.

Preheat the grill/barbecue to medium–high.

Grill the sardines for 5 minutes, then turn them over and grill for a further 5 minutes, until cooked. Lay the lemon slices on the grill/barbecue and cook until charred.

Plate the sardines and grilled lemons, drizzle with olive oil, season with salt and pepper, and serve.

12 sardines, gutted and cleaned

12 brined vine leaves

1 recipe of Black Olive Stuffing (see page 102)

2 lemons, cut into thick slices

olive oil, to drizzle

sea salt and cracked black pepper

SERVES 4

Chive Blossom BUTTER

1 bunch of chives with blossoms

2 sticks/225 g unsalted butter, at room temperature

sea salt and cracked black pepper

YIELDS ABOUT 1 CUP/240 G

Chive blossoms are so pretty and their pinky-lavender balls really add glamour to this butter. The delicate onion taste is a perfect match for anything. I like to make it to spread on warm cheese scones for a weekend treat.

Separate the chive blossoms from the stems. Roughly chop the blossoms and finely chop the stems.

Put the chopped stems and butter in a food processor and process until smooth. Stir in the blossoms and season with salt and pepper. Refrigerate until ready to use.

To make a butter roll, spoon the butter mixture onto a piece of plastic wrap/clingfilm. Fold the wrap/film over the butter and roll into a sausage shape. Twist the ends to secure and store in the fridge or freezer. When you're ready to use the butter, slice off discs as desired.

To use, melt over grilled fish and vegetables.

Meyer Lemon BUTTER

freshly squeezed juice and grated zest of 2 large Meyer lemons

2 sticks/225 g unsalted butter, at room temperature

a pinch of pink Himalayan salt

YIELDS 1 CUP/240 G

Meyer lemons are my absolute favorite citrus. I make tarts with them, preserve them, and squeeze them into anything I can get away with. Their yellow–orange skins are so pretty and fragrant. This butter is fantastic melted over fish of any description.

Put the lemon zest and juice, butter, and salt in a food processor and process until smooth. Refrigerate until ready to use.

To make a butter roll, spoon the butter mixture onto a piece of plastic wrap/clingfilm. Fold the wrap/film over the butter and roll into a sausage shape. Twist the ends to secure and store in the fridge or freezer. When you're ready to use the butter, slice off discs as desired.

To use, melt over grilled fish and vegetables.

Wasabi CREAM

2 tablepoons wasabi powder

1 cup/240 ml crème fraîche

sea salt and ground black pepper

YIELDS 1 CUP/240 ML

Wasabi is a Japanese ingredient most commonly used in sushi. It comes in a paste or powder. It really is a perfect way to dress something up, especially cream. You can make it spicier by adding more, but it boils down to personal taste.

Whisk together the wasabi powder and crème fraîche in a glass bowl and season with the salt and pepper.

Store in a glass container with a tight fitting-lid in the refrigerator for up to 1 week.

To use, melt over grilled fish and vegetables or serve with smoked salmon, smoked trout, and crab cakes.

Grilled LOBSTERS with TWO BUTTERS

My sister Elvena and I love lobsters and Champagne, it's our special treat. Where she lives in Scotland we are lucky enough to reap the benefits of the local and sustainable catch. First we boil them, then cut them in half and finish on the grill with lashings of flavored butters and, of course, serve them with icy cold bubbly.

Fill the stock pot three quarters full with water and add the salt. Bring to a boil and carefully add 2 of the lobsters. Cook for 10 minutes, then remove and place on a wooden cutting board. Cook the remaining 2 lobsters in the same way.

When the lobsters are cool enough to handle, cut them in half from head to tail using a sharp knife or scissors. Season well with salt and pepper.

Lay the lobster halves, cut side down, on a medium–high grill/barbecue and cook for 2–3 minutes. Turn them over and dot with the flavored butters. Continue to cook for a further 3–4 minutes, until the butter has melted.

Serve immediately with more butter, lemons, and ice cold Champagne.

2 teaspoons sea salt

4 lobsters (about 1½–2 lb./ 680–900 g each)

Chive Blossom Butter (see page 108)

Meyer Lemon Butter (see page 109)

sea salt and cracked black pepper

4 lemons, cut into quarters, to serve

a large stock or pasta pot

SERVES 4

VEGETABLES

There is a huge push for fresh farm to table produce, especially with vegetables. It seems everyone is growing their own. Whether it's growing a simple pot of tomatoes on a balcony, keeping a plot in an urban community, raising a roof top garden, or filling your back yard with produce, there is an enthusiastic movement that understands the difference in taste and the manner in which produce is being farmed. Sustainability is key and people want to buy fresh local produce that is organic and healthy.

Support your local farmers' market and shop there. It's wonderful to slowly meander through the stalls bulging with bright freshly picked vegetables in a rainbow of colors. The aromatics from the herbs and fruits fill the air with perfume and fill your senses. Build up relationships with the farmers and find out what their farming practices are. You will enjoy eating seasonally and know that the best things are worth waiting for. It is exciting after a long dark winter, to bite into a tall spear of green asparagus, which shouts it's spring again and the dark months seem far behind.

One of my all time favorite seasonal foods is Fried Green Tomatoes and I never get tired of them. When they appear at the market it seems I had almost forgotten about them but then I can't wait to get home and toss them in a spicy cornmeal mix and fry them up. Simple and timeless.

My friends always ask me for new ideas for cooking veggies. My answer is always the same, Grilled Market Vegetables. Never the same, the vegetables change from season to season, which is why you just don't get bored with it. Fantastic for outdoor cooking in the summer but even in the winter, when it's too cold to grill outside, you can simply cook on the stove top in a grill pan. All you have to do is pick your favorite veggies, toss them in a tangy dressing, and simply grill until slightly charred. Serve with breads lavishly spread with herbed butters. Healthy, light, quick, and so easy.

Vegetables can take on any kind of seasoning and this is what is so great about them. Pickling is one of the best ways to enjoy the seasonal harvest throughout the year, especially the summer harvest. The term "Put Ups" is fondly used for putting up (or preserving) the harvest to eat throughout the winter. I know preserving and pickling can make you fearful, but you can make pickles and simply store in the refrigerator for 2–3 weeks. Once you have mastered this, try out some different techniques for preserving for longer periods—it really is worth it.

Butter is in everyone's fridge. This wonderful pat of golden yellow can be flavored with absolutely anything you have in your pantry. Use dried herbs and spices or aromatic, leafy fresh herbs from the garden. All kinds of fruits can be used, such as apples, quinces, figs, peaches, and apricots. Chop in olives, pickles, and fiery chiles or zest up lemons, limes and oranges and stir in. Spoon savory butters through a hot bowl of rice, dollop on potatoes, or spread on fresh crusty bread and toast. Use fruit butters for spreading on freshly baked warm scones. The list is endless and that is what is fun about it.

Marinated GOAT CHEESE

8 oz./225 g goat cheese

1 lemon

4 bay leaves

½ teaspoon black peppercorns

½ teaspoon dried chili flakes

1 cup/240 ml extra virgin olive oil

a 1-quart/1-litre glass jar, sterilized (see page 4)

YIELDS 1 QUART/LITRE

At our local Sunday farmers' market, we head straight to the goat cheese stand as they have the most amazing cheeses suspended in delicious herbed oils. But the best part is that they always bring a baby goat with them. While the farmer stands cradling the goat in his arms, a multitude of people pet and gush at his cuteness and always the baby goat sleeps through the whole ordeal.

Roll the goat cheese into small balls.

Peel the lemon and cut the skin into strips. (You don't need the lemon flesh or juice, so reserve this for another use.)

Layer the goat cheese, lemon peel, bay leaves, peppercorns, and chili flakes in the prepared glass jar. Pour over the olive oil making sure to cover the goat cheese.

Store the cheese in the jar in the fridge for up to 2 months.

Use according to the recipe on page 118, or on a cheese board, pizzas, calzone, and pasta.

Fattoush MIX

1 tablespoon sumac

2 teaspoons dried mint

freshly squeezed juice and grated zest of 1 lemon

2 garlic cloves, finely chopped

2 tablespoons red wine vinegar

½ cup/120 ml extra virgin olive oil

sea salt and cracked black pepper

YIELDS ¾ CUP/180 ML

This is my version of the spice mix that is used in the famous Lebanese salad Fattoush, which means crumbled bread. Sumac is a coarse spice used in Mediterranean and Middle Eastern cooking—it has a wonderful bitter lemon taste.

Put all the ingredients in a bowl and mix together. Season with salt and pepper and cover until ready to use.

Store the fattoush in an airtight container in the fridge for up to 1 week.

Use the fattoush to dress salads or drizzle over vegetables, poultry, and meat before grilling.

Chow Chow SPICY BRINE

2 cups/480 ml apple cider vinegar

½ cup/100 g granulated/caster sugar

2 teaspoons ground turmeric

2 teaspoons ground ginger

2 teaspoons yellow mustard seeds

1 teaspoon mustard powder

1 teaspoon black peppercorns

1 teaspoon ground coriander

½ teaspoon curry powder

sterilized glass jars (see page 4)

YIELDS 2½ CUPS/600 ML

Turmeric is the main ingredient here, which gives Chow Chow a wonderful ochre color. It is a great way to preserve vegetables and the dazzling colors add glamour to any plate of food. I like to use this spicy brine to pickle cauliflowers, beans, asparagus, onions, and cabbage, but any vegetable can be used. I always think of it as the American South's version of British Piccalilli.

Put all the ingredients in a nonreactive saucepan and bring to a boil. Reduce the heat and simmer for about 5–8 minutes, until the sugar has dissolved, stirring occasionally.

Use for preserving vegetables. Tightly pack them into sterilized jars, pour in the hot brine, and seal. Store in a cool place for up to 1 year.

Caramelized
BEET TATIN

Don't think a tatin is only for apples and stone fruits. Here is a delicious, healthy, and savory turn of events using fresh beets as the star. Pair with an earthy, fresh herb like thyme and top it off with delicious marinated goat cheese dripping in olive oil and lemons. It's just the right size for a lunch party.

Preheat the oven to 425°F (220°C) Gas 7.

On a lightly floured work surface, dust the puff pastry with flour and cut out a circle 11-inch/28-cm in diameter.

Set the cast-iron pan over a medium–high heat, and melt the butter and maple syrup. Stir until combined and cook for about 5 minutes, until bubbling and caramelized.

Remove the pan from the heat and scatter 6 sprigs of thyme into the butter-syrup mixture. Arrange the beet slices in a layer of concentric circles covering the base of the pan, then return the pan to the heat and continue to cook for a further 5 minutes.

Lay the pastry on top of the beets, tucking in the overhanging edges, then transfer the pan to the preheated oven. Bake for 15 minutes until golden brown. Remove from the oven and leave to cool slightly. Carefully invert the tatin onto a serving plate.

Top with crumbled marinated goat cheese and some of the remaining thyme sprigs. Sprinkle with a little sea salt to finish.

13 oz./375 g ready-rolled puff pastry, thawed if frozen

1 tablespoon butter

1 tablespoon maple syrup

a handful of fresh thyme sprigs

4 red beets, peeled and thinly sliced

1 recipe of Marinated Goat Cheese (see page 116)

sea salt, to sprinkle

a 10-inch/25-cm cast iron pan

SERVES 4–6

"Put Ups" SUMMER PICKLE BRINE

2 cups/480 ml red wine vinegar

½ cup/100 g granulated/caster sugar

1 teaspoon black peppercorns

1 teaspoon yellow mustard seeds

1½ tablespoons sea salt

sterilized glass jars
(see page 4, optional)

YIELDS 2½ CUPS/600 ML

The term "Put Ups" makes me smile every time I hear it spoken. It is such a lovely term for putting up the harvest when the bounty is preserved for eating through the barren winter months. Nothing makes me happier than opening a jar of pickled summer vegetables in the midst of winter. Summer jumps straight out at you. Put Ups don't last long in our house—they seem to get devoured too quickly!

Put all the ingredients in a non-reactive saucepan and bring to a boil. Use as directed in the recipe on page 123, or as a preserving brine.

To preserve, pour the hot liquid over the tightly packed vegetables in sterilized glass jars and seal. Store in a cool place for up to 1 year.

Anchoïade BUTTER

1 stick/120 g unsalted butter,
at room temperature

2 oz./55 g can anchovies in oil

1 tablespoon chopped fresh flat-leaf parsley leaves

½ teaspoon herbes de Provence

freshly squeezed juice and grated zest of 1 lemon

Fleur de Sel and cracked black pepper

YIELDS ¾ CUP/200 G

This is a butter variation of the delicious Provençal dip. It's a bold little butter and holds up well to grilled meats and fish as well as vegetables. It is so quick to make and if you are a anchovy devotee you will love this. Simply spread it on thick slices of toasted rustic breads and eat.

Put all the ingredients, except for the salt and pepper, in a food procesosr and process until smooth but leaving a little texture in the butter. Season to taste with salt and pepper. Refrigerate until ready to use.

To make a butter roll, spoon the butter mixture onto a piece of plastic wrap/clingfilm. Fold the wrap/film over the butter and roll into a sausage shape. Twist the ends to secure and store in the fridge or freezer. When you're ready to use the butter, slice off discs as desired.

To use, melt over grilled vegetables, fish, and meat, or spread on breads.

Fried Green TOMATO SPICE MIX

1 cup/150 g fine-grain cornmeal

2 tablespoons coarse cornmeal/polenta

½ teaspoon cayenne pepper

½ teaspoon dried garlic powder

½ teaspoon dried chili flakes

1 teaspoon dried oregano

1 teaspoon dried basil

½ teaspoon ground black pepper

¼ teaspoon Kosher/table salt

YIELDS 1¼ CUPS/300 ML

This mix can be used for a lot of other dishes. I toss okra in it and have even been known to fry fish in a coat of this. The cornmeal adds a nice crunch against the cooked tomatoes while the Louisiana-style spices pack a flavor punch.

Put all the ingredients together in a bowl and mix together.

Store the spice mix in a glass jar with a tight-fitting lid for up to 1 month.

Use according to the recipe on page 123, or as preferred.

Fried GREEN
TOMATOES
with SUMMER PICKLES

This is a big taste of the South right here. Green tomatoes lightly tossed in a spicy cornmeal, then fried until crisp and golden brown. Served alongside a beautiful pile of summer pickles, there is nothing better. It's a meal in itself. Don't try to substitute ripe tomatoes —it just isn't the same.

To make the pickles, cut the vegetables into bite-size batons and layer in a ceramic baking dish. Pour over the hot "Put Ups" Summer Pickle Brine, cover, and set aside for 4–24 hours. When ready to eat, remove the vegetables from the brine and pile up in a serving bowl.

Wash the tomatoes under cold water and slice them into ½-inch/1-cm discs. Pour the Fried Green Tomato Spice Mix into a shallow bowl and lightly toss the tomato slices in it.

Heat a cast iron pan over a medium–high heat and coat with vegetable oil. Put a single layer of tomatoes in the pan and cook for about 3–5 minutes until golden brown. Turn the tomatoes over and continue to cook until crispy and golden brown. Remove the cooked tomatoes to a platter and continue to cook the remainder in batches. Sprinkle liberally with coarse sea salt and serve immediately with a bowl of the Summer Pickles.

6 large green tomatoes

1 recipe of Fried Green Tomato Spice Mix (see page 121)

vegetable oil, to cook

coarse sea salt, to sprinkle

SUMMER PICKLES

1 lb./450 g mixed summer vegetables, such as zucchini/courgette, beans, beets, and bell peppers

1 recipe of "Put Ups" Summer Pickle Brine (see page 120)

a cast iron pan

SERVES 4–6

Spanish SHERRY MARINADE

½ cup/120 ml extra virgin olive oil

¼ cup/60 ml Jerez Spanish vinegar

2 garlic cloves, finely chopped

1 shallot, finely chopped

a pinch of Spanish smoked paprika (pimentòn)

coarse sea salt and cracked black pepper

YIELDS SCANT 1 CUP/200 ML

If there is one ingredient that I am passionate about, it is Spanish sherry vinegar. My favorites come from the town of Jerez de la Frontera. They are strong and heady and add vibrancy to any foods. Apart from marinades and vinaigrettes, I drizzle them on cooked meats and fish for that last surprise of taste.

Put all the ingredients in a bowl and mix together.

Store the marinade in a glass jar in the refrigerator for up to 1 month.

Use according to the recipe on page 126, or to drizzle over roasted vegetables, or use in salads such as panzanella.

Garden HERB BUTTER

1 stick/120 g unsalted butter, at room temperature

2 generous tablespoons fresh oregano leaves

2 generous tablespoons fresh marjoram leaves

2 generous tablespoons fresh thyme leaves

1 generous tablespoon fresh rosemary leaves

Sel de Gris and ground black pepper

YIELDS GENEROUS ½ CUP/130 G

This is a wonderful green butter that just says it all. Fresh from the garden or farmers' market, make sure you use freshly picked herbs. Don't freeze this butter as the herbs tend to go black and lose their flavor. Spread it on breads or scones and dollop on top of roasted vegetables to add a whole new spin.

Put all the ingredients in a food processor and process until smooth but leaving a little texture in the butter. Refrigerate until ready to use.

To make a butter roll, spoon the butter mixture onto a piece of plastic wrap/clingfilm. Fold the wrap/film over the butter and roll into a sausage shape. Twist the ends to secure and store in the fridge. When you're ready to use the butter, slice off discs as desired.

To use, melt over grilled vegetables or spread on breads.

Green Tapenade BUTTER

2 sticks/225 g unsalted butter,
at room temperature

½ cup/50 g Lucques or green
olives, pitted

1 garlic clove, roughly chopped

1 tablespoon salted capers

a small bunch of fresh flat-leaf
parsley, roughly chopped

cracked black pepper

YIELDS 1½ CUPS/300 G

I use Lucques olives for this butter, but any good quality green olive will do. Matched with salty capers, this butter is to be dolloped extravagantly on anything hot, straight off the grill.

Put all the ingredients in a food processor and process until smooth but leaving a little texture in the butter. Refrigerate until ready to use.

To make a butter roll, spoon the butter mixture onto a piece of plastic wrap/clingfilm. Fold the wrap/film over the butter and roll into a sausage shape. Twist the ends to secure and store in the fridge or freezer. When you're ready to use the butter, slice off discs as desired.

To use, melt over grilled vegetables, meat, or fish or spread on breads.

Grilled MARKET
VEGETABLE SALAD
with HERBED TOASTS

1 head Radicchio Treviso, quartered

1 head Romaine/cos lettuce, quartered

2 small fennel, with fronds, quartered

6 zucchini/courgettes halved

1 cup/160 g cherry tomatoes

6 Japanese eggplant/aubergine, halved

1 recipe of Spanish Sherry Marinade
(see page 124)

coarse sea salt, to sprinkle

extra virgin olive oil, to drizzle

a handful of freshly torn flat-leaf
parsley, to garnish

HERBED TOASTS

1 large baguette, thickly sliced

1 recipe of Garden Herb Butter
(see page 124)

SERVES 6—8

This recipe is just ripe for a visit to the farmers' market, when you come home laden with a kaleidoscope of colorful vegetables. Follow the suggestions below or make up your own choice. It can be a combination of anything from tomatoes to squash to celery. Pile the beautifully charred vegetables onto a large wooden board with grilled toasts and serve. Simple outdoor summer grilling and eating at its best.

Put all the vegetables in a large ceramic baking dish and pour over the Spanish Sherry Marinade. Toss to cover well and set aside.

Spread a generous amount of Garden Herb Butter on both sides of the baguette slices and set aside.

Heat the grill/barbecue to medium. In batches, grill the vegetables, turning them over, until slightly charred all over. Some vegetables will cook quicker than others so remove these from the grill/barbecue as they are cooked. Transfer the vegetables to a large wooden board and dress lightly with any remaining marinade.

Grill the baguette slices until well toasted and place on the board alongside the vegetables. Sprinkle generously with the coarse sea salt, drizzle with olive oil, and garnish with fresh parsley, to serve.

DESSERTS

Go wild seasoning desserts: jazz up apple pies by simply adding a sprinkle of caraway seeds or crumble herbs into pastry to give a savory flair to a wonderful sweet summer peach or plum tart.

Research the area where you live and find out about picking your own fruit. It is a great activity to do with friends, family, and especially children. There are a lot of good farms that offer this opportunity, and you are guaranteed to be enjoying wonderful organic produce and the true farm to table experience. Come home with your pick and make preserves, pies, and tarts. Imagine, in the depth of winter, opening your pantry and reaching for a jar of sweet peaches that you poached and preserved with a spice mix. It's sunshine from the summer and will guarantee to make you smile.

Summertime is when to make the most of trying out new recipes. The markets are at their best, spilling over with a rich array of vibrant colors and heady fragrances from the seasonal fruit. Because there is so much fruit around, you can be adventurous and try out new recipes, such as Perfumed Poached Peaches that have been cooked in a floral Elderflower poaching liquid. Or take freshly picked raspberries and strawberries and macerate them in perfumed Lemongrass Syrup. Serve these summer bounties with creams that you have flavored with spices, liquors, perfumed waters, or herbs. They make a magnificent match.

Summer is also the time for lots of outdoor activities and eating. Rocky Road Campfire S'mores really round off the evening when everyone is sitting around relaxed and chatting and the last embers of the fire are glowing. This is the best time to cook marshmallows, then mash them between two freshly baked ginger cookies along with chunks of chocolate. Heavenly flavors of the marshmallow, chocolate, and the ginger spices come together in every bite.

In fall, come all the wonderful apples, quinces, pears, pomegranates, and persimmons with their autumnal colors. Great for spicing and poaching and cooking in flavored syrups. Make pies and fruit breads then sprinkle them with sugars spiced with cinnamon, ginger, allspice, and rosemary.

As the weather turns cooler you want to be in the kitchen baking and making breads. Make a batch of Apple Pie Butter—it is wonderful spread on warm scones or dolloped on a stack of freshly baked pancakes or waffles. You can easily swap out the apple in this recipe and use pears or quinces. Or make all three and give your guests or family a weekend feast. These butters store very well in the freezer.

All of the short recipes in this chapter can be made ahead of time and stored in the refrigerator in glass or ceramic dishes with tight-fitting lids. Sugars and spice mixes store in glass jars, again with tight-fitting lids, in your pantry where it is cool and dark. They will last up to 6 months, then after that the spices tend to lose their aromatics.

You can also flavor vodka, gin, and tequila with herbs and spices. Add fresh lime leaves to a bottle of tequila and let it marinade for a month—it will add a floral flavor to margaritas—or pop a few fresh chiles in a bottle of vodka to spice up bloody mary's. Add fruit or citrus to liquors and enjoy a fruity digestif. Other great choices for flavoring are vanilla beans, star anise, chili flakes, cinnamon sticks, bay leaves, and cardamom pods.

French SPICE MIX

1½ teaspoons ground ginger

½ teaspoon ground cinnamon

½ teaspoon ground allspice

½ teaspoon ground anise

¼ teaspoon ground cloves

YIELDS 2 TABLESPOONS

Hands down, pain d'espices is one of my favorite spiced cakes—not too sweet and the perfect partner for an afternoon cup of tea, or toasted for breakfast loaded with salty butter. It's the French equivalent of gingerbread and this is the classsic spice mix used.

Put all the ingredients in a bowl and mix together.

Store the spice mix in a glass jar with a tight-fitting lid for up to 6 months.

To use, add the spice mix to cakes, scones and cookies.

Lemongrass POACHING SYRUP

1 stalk fresh lemongrass

1 cup/200 g granulated/caster sugar

YIELDS 2 CUPS/500 ML

I like to keep a jar of this wonderful fragrant syrup in the fridge. It's great for all kind of fruits, homemade lemonade, and drizzling over ice creams and sorbets. You could also try flavoring the syrup with rosemary, lemon verbena, tarragon, or rose geranium—they are all delicious.

Chop the lemon grass stalk into large chunks and bruise them with the back of your knife blade to release the oils.

Put all the ingredients in a non-reactive pan with 2 cups/480 ml water and set over a medium–high heat. Bring to a boil, then reduce the heat to medium–low. Simmer for about 5–8 minutes, until the sugar dissolves. Remove from the heat and allow the syrup to cool completely.

When cool, strain the syrup into an airtight container and store in the fridge for up to 2 weeks.

To use, put the fruit in a bowl and pour over the poaching syrup. You can also use this to flavor cocktails.

Rose CREAM

1 cup/240 ml heavy/double cream

1 tablespoon granulated/caster sugar

a few drops of rosewater

YIELDS 1 CUP/240 ML

Rosewater is a dreamy essence that is used a lot in Middle Eastern cooking. It perfumes food with a wonderful tone. When I make strawberry jam, I always add a few drops and people always ask me what the secret ingredient is. Here I have infused cream with it, which you can dollop on desserts or serve with scones and jam for afternoon tea.

Pour the cream into a bowl and beat with an electric hand whisk until thickened. Fold in the sugar, add a few drops of rosewater, and stir to combine. Cover and refrigerate until ready to use.

Elderflower POACHING WINE

1 cup/240 ml St Germain

3 fresh bay leaves, bruised

2 large sprigs fresh lemon verbena

2 teaspoons granulated/caster sugar

YIELDS 1 CUP/240 ML

St Germain is a French liquor made with the blossoms of elderflowers picked in the Alps. Everyone should have a bottle on their shelves. It's heavenly scented and perfect for cocktails, or add a dash to a glass of Champagne. It makes poached fruits sing!

Put all the ingredients in a non-reactive pan with 3 cups/700 ml water and set over a medium–high heat. Bring to a boil, then reduce the heat to medium–low and simmer for about 5–8 minutes, until the sugar dissolves. Leave to cool, then strain.

To use, follow the recipe on page 135, adjusting the cooking time up or down according to which fruits you are poaching.

Lemongrass
SUMMER BERRIES
with ROSE CREAM

4 cups/500 g raspberries

2 cups/230 g strawberries

1 recipe of Lemongrass Poaching Syrup (see page 132)

lemon verbena, to garnish (optional)

1 recipe of Rose Cream (see page 133), to serve

SERVES 4—6

Nothing in the world shouts "summer" better than fresh strawberries and raspberries. Picked sweet and juicy they need very little to dress them up. Lemongrass perfumes the fruits and the floral rose cream turns the dish into a bouquet of flavors. Try and eat this slowly and savor, although I know it's hard to do.

Rinse the berries under cold water and hull the strawberries.

Put the berries in a serving dish and pour over the lemongrass syrup. Allow to marinate for 1—4 hours.

Garnish with lemon verbena and serve with lots of rose cream.

Perfumed POACHED
PEACHES

A stunningly beautiful dessert, filled with simplicity and heady aromatics for a hot summer evening. I serve it chilled with a sprinkling of tiny flowers, such as borage, strawberry, rose petals, or even some herbs—whatever you have handy in the garden.

Put the peaches in a non-reactive pan and pour over the Elderflower Poaching Wine. Bring to a boil on a medium–high heat, then reduce to a lively simmer and cook for 8–10 minutes—you want the peaches to be to be cooked but still hold their shape. Remove the peaches with a slotted spoon, put on a plate, and set aside to cool.

Increase the heat under the pan and simmer the poaching liquid to reduce by half—this should take about 5 minutes—then turn off the heat and allow to cool.

Peel the peaches and place each one in a bowl. Drizzle with the cooled syrup. Sprinkle with flowers and serve with mascarpone.

COOK'S NOTE: I like to chill the peaches and syrup in the fridge until ready to serve. This can be made a day ahead.

4 sweet firm ripe peaches

1 recipe of Elderflower Poaching Wine (see page 133)

small edible flowers, to garnish (optional)

mascarpone, to serve

SERVES 4

Italian Dessert POACHING WINE

1 cup/240 ml good Italian dessert wine

1 vanilla bean/pod, split in half

2 teaspoons brown sugar

YIELDS 1 CUP/250 ML

I'm using an Italian dessert wine but you can absolutely use any kind of sweet wine, such as a Reisling. This is such a simple way to flavor fruit, especially if a little unripe. A versatile poaching wine, that can be used for any fruits.

Put all the ingredients in a non-reactive saucepan set over a medium–high heat. Bring to a boil, then immediately reduce the heat to a simmer. Cook for about 5–6 minutes, until the sugar is dissolved, then leave to cool.

Store in an airtight container in the fridge for up to 1 week.

To use, follow the recipe on page 139, adjusting the cooking time up or down according to which fruits you are poaching.

Orange CREAM

1 cup/240 ml crème fraîche

grated zest of 1 orange

1 tablespoon orange blossom honey

3 tablespoons orange liqueur, such as Grand Mariner or Cointreau

YIELDS 1¼ CUPS/300 ML

Flavoring creams and yogurts can add a delicious layer to desserts. You can use fruits, spices, herbs, and wines to do it. Just have fun experimenting. You will not be disappointed.

Put all the ingredients in a glass bowl and whisk together. Cover and refrigerate until ready to use.

Store the cream in the refrigerator for up to 1 week.

Serve on the side of desserts, such as tarts and poached fruits, or with scones and breads.

Ginger Spiced SUGAR

⅓ cup/65 g cane sugar (or use any sugar of your choice)

2 tablespoons ground ginger

YIELDS GENEROUS ⅓ CUP/80 G

Season all kinds of sugar with spices or dried herbs and add to a dessert or stir into a morning cup of coffee to brighten your day. I keep my vanilla beans in my sugar canister, which adds great flavor when baking.

Put all the ingredients into a small glass jar. Screw on the lid and vigorously shake.

Store the sugar in a glass jar with a tight-fitting lid for up to 6 months.

To use, sprinkle on baked desserts, crepes, and roasted fruits.

Apple Pie BUTTER

2 small to medium apples, skin on, cored and roughly chopped

½ cup/120 ml apple juice

½ cup/120 ml water

1 cinnamon stick

1 teaspoon apple pie spice/mixed spice

¼ cup/60 ml maple syrup

1 tablespoon Calvados (optional)

2 sticks/225 g butter, at room temperature

YIELDS ABOUT 2 CUPS/500 G

Fresh butter laced with apples and spices is perfect for fall when the weather has turned cool and you want to spread something special on freshly baked scones or toast. I also use it in abundance when making bread and butter pudding, adding a dash of Calvados.

Put the apples, cider, cinnamon stick and apple pie spice/mixed spice in a non-reactive pan with ½ cup/120 ml water. Cover and bring to a boil over a medium–high heat. Reduce the heat and simmer the apples for 15–20 minutes, breaking up and mashing the apples with the back of a wooden spoon. Remove from the heat and discard the cinnamon stick. Pour in the maple syrup and Calvados, if using, and mix thoroughly. Set aside to cool.

When cool, put the apple mixture and butter in a food processor and process until you have a coarse butter. Refrigerate until ready to use.

To make a butter roll, spoon the butter mixture onto a piece of plastic wrap/clingfilm. Fold the wrap/film over the butter and roll into a sausage shape. Twist the ends to secure and store in the fridge or freezer. When you're ready to use the butter, slice off discs as desired.

To use, spread on freshly baked scones and breads.

Sozzled APRICOT
BRUSCHETTA
with ORANGE CREAM

This is a show stopper, believe me. Grilled panettone topped with sozzled apricots, lavishly dolloped with orange cream and a decadent drizzle of honey. It is the most delicious dessert to serve when apricots are in season. If there are any leftover sozzled apricots, store in the fridge and have with cheeses or stir into yogurt.

Put the apricot halves in a non-reactive pan and add the Italian Dessert Poaching Wine. Set the pan over a medium–high heat and bring to a boil, then reduce the heat to medium–low and simmer for 10 minutes. You want the apricots to cook but still hold a little of their shape.

Remove the apricots from the pan with a slotted spoon and put in a ceramic bowl. Turn the heat back up to medium–high and simmer for about 5 minutes to reduce the poaching liquid by half, stirring frequently. Pour the syrup over the apricots.

Heat a gas or charcoal grill/barbecue to medium–high heat, or place a grill pan on the stove top over medium–high heat.

Grill the panettone or brioche slices for about 2 minutes per side, until toasted. Place each one on a plate and spoon the sozzled apricots, along with the juices, over each slice of toasted panettone. Dollop with the orange cream, drizzle with honey, and serve.

1½ lb./680 g (about 18) ripe apricots, halved and pitted

1 recipe of Italian Dessert Poaching Wine (see page 136)

6 slices panettone or brioche, about 1½ inches/4 cm thick

1 recipe of Orange Cream (see page 136)

honey, to drizzle

SERVES 6

Rocky ROAD
CAMPFIRE S'MORES
with GINGER SPICED SUGAR

COOKIES

1½ cups/200 g all-purpose/plain flour

½ teaspoon baking soda/bicarbonate of soda

½ teaspoon baking powder

1 recipe of French Spice Mix (see page 132)

a pinch of sea salt

1½ sticks/175 g unsalted butter, at room temperature

¾ cup/150 g dark brown sugar

1 egg

1 teaspoon vanilla extract

S'MORES

Ginger Spiced Sugar (see page 137)

a large bag of marshmallows

a large bar of plain chocolate

a large bar of milk chocolate

a baking sheet lined with baking parchment

long metal skewers or twigs

SERVES 6

Everyone in America knows the fun of making s'mores —they are a classic campfire food. Here I have matched spicy ginger cookies with chocolate, marshmallow, and more ginger spiced sugar to make a mouthwatering delight. Easy to make and even easier to eat!

In a mixing bowl, combine the flour, baking soda/bicarbonate of soda, baking powder, French Spice Mix, and sea salt and set aside.

In a separate mixing bowl, cream together the butter and brown sugar with an electric hand mixer until fluffy, then beat in the egg and vanilla extract. Slowly beat in the flour mixture until it forms a dough.

Tip the dough onto a sheet of plastic wrap/clingfilm and roll up into a log. Put in the freezer for 20 minutes.

Preheat the oven to 350°F (180°C) Gas 4.

Remove the dough from the freezer and slice the log into ¼-inch/½-cm discs. Arrange the discs on the prepared baking sheet and bake in the preheated oven for 10 minutes. Remove from the oven and sprinkle with the Ginger Spiced Sugar, then return to the oven and bake for a further 5 minutes. Remove from the oven and leave to cool on a wire rack.

To make the s'mores, thread marshmallows onto the skewers and toast over a fire. Sandwich them between the ginger cookies along with a piece of chocolate and eat.

SOURCES

ABESMARKET.COM
www.abesmarket.com

US online stockist selling a huge range of dried herbs, spices and seasonings as well as other natural foods.

KALUSTYAN'S
www.kalustyans.com

123 Lexington Avenue, New York, NY 10016
Tel: +1 (212) 685-3451

Manhattan spice market packed with unusual ingredients sourced from all over the globe.

MCCALL'S MEAT AND FISH COMPANY
www.mccallsmeatandfish.com

2117 Hillhurst Avenue, Los Angeles, CA 90027
Tel: +1 (323) 667-0674

Market selling premium meat and fish in Los Angeles.

MOUNTAIN ROSE HERBS
www.mountainroseherbs.com

US online shop selling high-quality organic herbs and spices.

ORGANIC SPICES
www.organicspices.com

US online shop selling high-quality organic herbs and spices.

SAHADI'S
www.sahadis.com

187 Atlantic Avenue, Brooklyn, New York, NY 11201
Tel: +1 (718) 624-4550

Dry goods emporium with a huge array of international ingredients, including bulk bins of spices, nuts, grains, dry fruit and olives from around the world.

SEASONED PIONEERS
www.seasonedpioneers.co.uk

UK online shop selling high-quality organic herbs and spices.

THE SPICE HOUSE
www.thespicehouse.com

US purveyor of spices, available in their online shop or in stores in Illinois and Wisconsin – visit website for addresses.

THE SPICE LAB INC.
www.thespicelab.com

US online purveyor of artisan salts and spices from around the world.

SPICE MOUNTAIN
www.spicemountain.co.uk

UK online stockist selling a huge range of spices.

THE SPICE SHOP
www.thespiceshop.co.uk

1 Blenheim Crescent, London, W11 2EE
Tel: +44 (0) 207 221 4448

Long-established London spice shop offering a range of over 2,500 products, including their own blends and mixes.

SPICE STATION SILVERLAKE
www.spicestationsilverlake.com

3819 West Sunset Boulevard, Los Angeles, CA 90026 Tel: +1 (323) 660-2565

Gourmet spice shop with branches in Santa Monica and Silverlake, offering over 200 spices, herbs, chiles, salts and blends from around the world.

STARWEST BOTANICALS
www.starwest-botanicals.com

US online shop selling bulk organic herbs and spices as well as their own seasoning blends.

STEENBERGS ORGANICS
www.steenbergs.co.uk

UK purveyor of organic Fairtrade spices and other cooking ingredients. Buy online or visit their website for details of local stockists.

INDEX

ACKNOWLEDGMENTS

Thank you to Leslie Harrington and Julia Charles for asking me to write and style *Smoke and Spice*—it has been such a great project and my kitchen has smelt like a wonderful perfumed souk while I have been cooking up a storm. Thanks to Rebecca Woods for happily guiding me through and Geoff Borin for the beautiful design. Huge thanks to the very talented photographer Erin Kunkel, who shot the whole thing and was a lot of fun to have around. She made it very easy. Thank you Sandra for happily running the kitchen and keeping me straight! My sister Elvena (and her company E. A. Alvarino Antiques, Scotland) for all the lovely cutlery and antique cookware you have given me over the years—I cherish it all and love you, thank you for leading the way. Jennifer Barguiarena for her wonderful props and laughter. My husband who happily ate his way through everything, thank you for all the love and laughter.

VALERIE AIKMAN-SMITH

Valerie Aikman-Smith is a food stylist, chef and cookbook author based in Los Angeles. She first cooked in San Francisco and then segued her skills into food styling and writing.

Her work includes international assignments for magazines and she has cooked and styled her way through the Greek Islands, Paris, Mexico, Croatia, Scotland and the U.S.A. Additionally, her work is seen in many cookbooks, commercials, print and advertising campaigns as well as Television and Film.

Valerie is the author and stylist of the cookbooks *Salt*, published by Ryland Peters & Small, and *Cooking with Cast Iron* and *Juicy Drinks* for Williams Sonoma.